IT Asset Management Foundation (ITAMF) Workbook - Second edition

Other publications by Van Haren Publishing

Van Haren Publishing (VHP) specializes in titles on Best Practices, methods and standards within four domains:
- IT and IT Management
- Architecture (Enterprise and IT)
- Business Management and
- Project Management

Van Haren Publishing is also publishing on behalf of leading organizations and companies: ASLBiSL Foundation, BRMI, CA, Centre Henri Tudor, CATS CM, Gaming Works, IACCM, IAOP, IFDC, Innovation Value Institute, IPMA-NL, ITSqc, NAF, KNVI, PMI-NL, PON, The Open Group, The SOX Institute.

Topics are (per domain):

IT and IT Management	Enterprise Architecture	Project Management
ABC of ICT	ArchiMate®	A4-Projectmanagement
ASL®	GEA®	DSDM/Atern
CMMI®	Novius Architectuur	ICB / NCB
COBIT®	Methode	ISO 21500
e-CF	TOGAF®	MINCE®
ISO/IEC 20000		M_o_R®
ISO/IEC 27001/27002	**Business Management**	MSP®
ISPL	BABOK® Guide	P3O®
IT4IT®	BiSL® and BiSL® Next	PMBOK® Guide
IT-CMF™	BRMBOK™	Praxis®
IT Service CMM	BTF	PRINCE2®
ITIL®	CATS CM®	
MOF	EFQM	
MSF	eSCM	
SABSA	IACCM	
SAF	ISA-95	
SIAM™	ISO 9000/9001	
TRIM	OPBOK	
VeriSM™	SixSigma	
	SOX	
	SqEME®	

For the latest information on VHP publications, visit our website: www.vanharen.net.

IT ASSET MANAGEMENT FOUNDATION (ITAMF)

Workbook - Second edition

Jan Øberg

Colophon

Title:	IT Asset Management Foundation (ITAMF) – Workbook Second edition
Author:	Jan Øberg
Publisher:	Van Haren Publishing, 's-Hertogenbosch-NL, www.vanharen.net.
ISBN Hard copy:	978 94 018 0716 6
ISBN eBook (pdf):	978 94 018 0717 3
ISBN ePUB:	978 94 018 0718 0
Edition:	Second edition, first impression, November 2020
Layout and Design:	Coco Bookmedia, Amersfoort-NL
Copyright:	© ITAMOrg and Van Haren Publishing, 2014, 2020

For more information about Van Haren Publishing, email us at: info@vanharen.net.

Copyright Notices
ITIL® is a registered trademark of AXELOS Limited.
ISO® is a registered trademark of the International Organization for Standardization.
COBIT® is a registered trademark of ISACA (previously known as the Information Systems Audit and Control Association).

No part of this publication may be reproduced in any form including printing, photocopying, microfilm or any other means without written permission by the publisher.
Although this publication has been compiled with great care, neither the author(s) nor the publisher accepts any liability for damages caused by any errors and/or imperfections in this publication.

Table of content

List of figures and diagrams...VII
Introduction..IX

1 INTRODUCTION TO IT ASSET MANAGEMENT (ITAM)................1

    1.1   Definition and goal of ITAM...1
    1.2   Standards and best practicEs.......................................6
    1.3   ITAM models..9
    Exam preparation: Chapter 1..11

2 HARDWARE ASSET MANAGEMENT (HAM).......................15

    2.1   Introduction to HAM..15
    2.2   Identification and management of hardware assets..................17
    2.3   Best practices, tools and mobile devices...........................22
    Exam preparation: Chapter 2..25

3 SOFTWARE ASSET MANAGEMENT (SAM).......................29

    3.1   Definition and objectives of SAM..................................29
    3.2   The concept of compliance..36
    3.3   The risks and costs related to software audits.....................37
    Exam preparation: Chapter 3..39

4 SERVICES AND CLOUD ASSET MANAGEMENT (SEAM)............43

    4.1   Definition and objectives of SEAM.................................43
    4.2   The concept of Services and cloud computing......................45
    4.3   The practice of SEAM...47
    4.4   Contracts and contract negotiation in SEAM........................49
    Exam preparation: Chapter 4..52

5 PEOPLE AND INFORMATION ASSET MANAGEMENT (PINAM) 55
    5.1   Definition and objectives of PINAM 55
    5.2   The guiding principles of PINAM 57
    5.3   The practice of PINAM 59
    5.4   Services and cloud: BYOD (Bring Your Own Device) 62
    Exam preparation: Chapter 5 64

6 IT ASSET MANAGEMENT INTERFACES 67
    6.1   The interfaces of IT Asset Management 67
    6.2   IT Asset Management roles 70
    Exam preparation: Chapter 6 73

Appendix A List of basic concepts. 75
Appendix B About ITAMOrg 77
Appendix C Answer Key 79

List of figures and diagrams

Figure 1. The ITAM lifecycle 1
Figure 2. Positioning of ITAM 2
Figure 3. ITAM ECO system stakeholder map 4
Figure 4. The ITAM 'Bermuda Triangle' 5
Figure 5. ITAM best practices 6
Figure 6. ITAM requirements for the management of assets 8
Figure 7. ITAM basic management system 8
Figure 8. ITAM process framework 9
Figure 9. The HAM lifecycle 17
Figure 10. Hardware Asset Management stakeholders 18
Figure 11. The hardware lifecycle process 22
Figure 12. SAM stakeholder map 32
Figure 13. SAM implementation roadmap 34
Figure 14. SAM tiered approach 35
Figure 15. SEAM 'Triple Play' 47
Figure 16. SEAM lifecycle 48
Figure 17. SEAM and the worlds of the internal and external IT provider 50
Figure 18. PINAM and the other ITAM areas 56
Figure 19. PINAM areas for attention 57
Figure 20. ITAM ECO system and alignment 67
Figure 21. ITAM interface approach 68
Figure 22. IT Asset Manager's central role 70
Figure 23. Daily operations involving assets 71
Figure 24. IT Asset Manager challenges 71
Figure 25. Challenges of related roles 72

Introduction

IT Asset Management Foundation (ITAMF) is a certification that validates a professional's knowledge on managing the IT assets as part of an organization's strategy, compliance and risk management. The content covered by the certification is based upon the philosophy of ITAMOrg, a membership organization and thought leader in IT Asset Management.

The certificate IT Asset Management Foundation is part of the ITAMOrg qualification program and has been developed in cooperation with international experts in the field.

This workbook will help you prepare for the IT Asset Management Foundation (ITAMF) exam and provides you with an overview of the four key areas of IT Asset Management: Hardware Asset Management, including 'mobile devices'; Software Asset Management; Services & Cloud Asset Management and People & Information Asset Management, including 'Bring Your Own Device' (BYOD).

The exam consists of 40 multiple choice questions with a pass mark of 65%. In this workbook, you will find several sample multiple choice questions, and to help increase your knowledge about IT Asset Management we have also included so-called 'get it' questions. You will find these questions at the end of each chapter. The exam requirements are specified at the beginning of each chapter, and the weight of the different exam topics is expressed as a percentage of the total.

ITAMOrg exam context

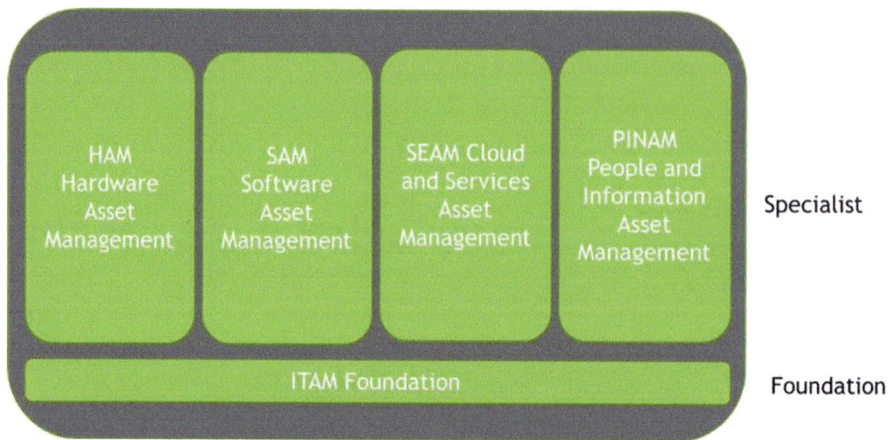

Source: ITAMOrg IT Asset Management Foundation preparation guide

Target group
IT Asset Management Foundation is intended for all key personnel in the organization involved in the IT lifecycle. Whilst this certification has an IT focus, it has been specifically designed for non-IT personnel in mind.

Specific roles/responsibilities could include (but are not limited to):
- General/business management
- IT manager
- Procurement manager
- Financial manager
- IT operations manager
- Project manager
- Process manager
- Contract manager
- Risk manager
- Business continuity manager
- Security manager

Competences
e-Competence Framework (e-CF)

e-CF Area		e-Competence	Level	Coverage
BUILD	B.5	Documentation Production	e-1	Superficial
ENABLE	D.4	Purchasing	e-2	Superficial
	D.8	Contract Management	e-2	Partial
MANAGE	E.3	Risk Management	e-3	Partial
	E.4	Relationship Management	e-3	Superficial
	E.5	Process Improvement	e-3	Superficial
	E.6	ICT Quality Management	e-2	Superficial
	E.8	Information Security Management	e-2	Superficial

Introduction to IT Asset Management (ITAM): Exam requirements

1. Introduction to IT Asset Management (ITAM)	10%
1.1 Definition and goal of ITAM	
1.2 Standards and best practices	
1.3 ITAM models	

1 Introduction to IT Asset Management (ITAM)

■ 1.1 DEFINITION AND GOAL OF ITAM

1.1.1 Defining ITAM

Information Technology Asset Management (ITAM) is the strategic management of IT-related assets throughout their lifecycles and is compiled of several best practice and business practices.

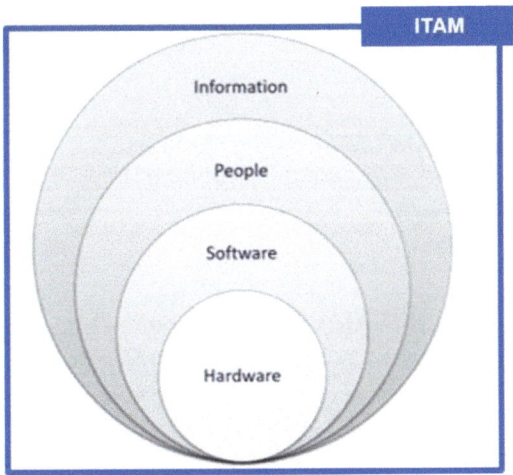

Figure 1. The ITAM lifecycle

ITAM is a set of business practices aligning financial, contractual and inventory areas to support the strategic decisions for the IT environment.

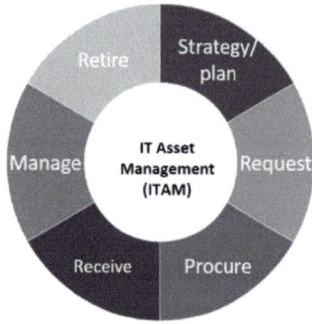

> IT assets are all aspects of Technologies: software, hardware, people and information (documentation such as contracts and services) used in a business.
>
> Information Technology Asset Management (ITAM) is divided in four key areas:
> **Hardware Asset Management (HAM):** Management of the physical components of computers, mobile devices and networks from acquisition, implementation, process adjustments, deployment to disposal.
>
> **Software Asset Management (SAM):** Managing the complete lifecycle of every software asset, involving cost control, documentation, licensing, redistribution, maintenance, etc.
>
> **Service and Cloud Asset Management (SEAM):** SEAM is the management of the multiple platforms across physical, virtual and cloud environments with respect to the organizational needs in terms of storage, data protection, policies and availability.
>
> **People & Information Asset Management (PINAM):** This discipline regards both people and information (data) as assets. The management of People and Information refers to data security, access policies and best practices with regard to knowledge and information sharing.

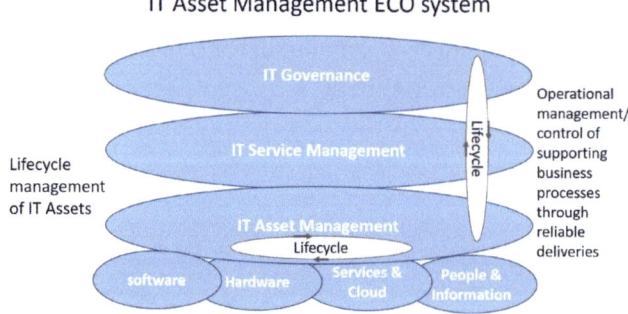

Figure 2. Positioning of ITAM

1 Introduction to IT Asset Management (ITAM)

In the IT Asset Management ECO system, the best practice process framework closest to IT Asset Management (ITAM) is IT Service Management (ITSM: i.e. ITIL® & ISO/IEC 20000).

1.1.2 The purpose and objectives of ITAM

The four key objectives of IT Asset Management are value creation, alignment, leadership and assurance.

Value creation
Principles that support staying in compliance, i.e. 'avoiding value destruction' are: risk management, effectiveness, efficiency, value innovation and avoiding disruptive change.

Leadership
Principles that support leadership are: promoting a positive workplace culture, define clear roles and responsibilities (including matching authorities), creating awareness and involvement of all stakeholders.

Assurance
It needs to be made clear that assets fulfill a purpose and are connected to organizational objectives. This must be supported by implementing proper processes, embracing the principle of continual improvement and providing necessary resources.

Alignment
Alignment is made possible by creating an IT Asset Management ECO system. The best practice process framework that is closest to ITAM, and has many overlap areas with ITAM is IT Service Management (ITSM).

Benefits
The benefits of Information Technology Asset Management are:
- Improving the efficiency of existing resources;
- Financial management of IT assets;
- Information security;
- Compliance with legislation, regulations and standards;
- Creating awareness of IT business and strategy;
- Enable knowledge and decision making based on up-to-date information;
- Goals, motivations and drivers of in- and external stakeholders.

ITAM stakeholders: who needs to be involved?
For ITAM to become successful it is key to involve stakeholders across the organization, and on all levels. Examples of ITAM stakeholders are: business and IT management, legal and commercial, procurement, the financial department, IT operations and

'last but not least' end-users. Creating awareness and sharing knowledge with all stakeholders is indispensable. There also needs to be a good balance between the IT asset strategy and the needs of the organization. ITAM helps to overcome typical issues, such as having no long-time planning causing unnecessary expenses.

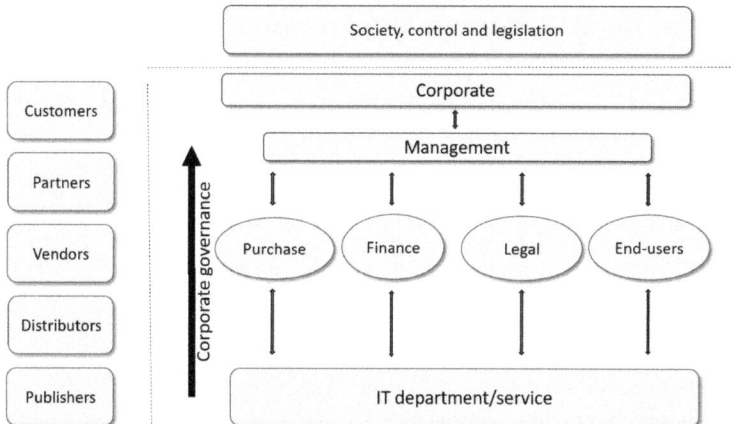

Figure 3. ITAM ECO system stakeholder map

Apart from all internal stakeholders mentioned above there are also various external stakeholders. Modern organizations are not isolated from the world. Apart from the obvious ones such as vendors and customers we also need to consider (local) government (general legislation) and governmental authorities governing all kinds of regulations. Furthermore, society has expectations with regard of the environment and social entrepreneurship. Figure 3 provides a concise map of stakeholders.

The 'Bermuda Triangle' of ITAM

In the section above we have seen that cooperation between stakeholders is a crucial aspect of ITAM. Another one is maintaining a balance between Requests, Purchasing and Deployment of assets. In ITAM this is called the 'Bermuda Triangle'. The three areas mentioned here are governed by different departments or stakeholders, each with their own objectives and needs. When ITAM does not control the interaction between the three, a nasty storm may start brewing within the organization and 'sink' the ITAM ship

Table 1. Stakeholder roles and responsibilities (summary)

Stakeholder	Focus areas
Society	Legislation, regulations, directives, environment
Board of directors / corporate governance	Owners/shareholders, strategy/mission/vision, long term business planning, business value, financial, corporate governance
Management	Budgets/specific financial goals, implementation of strategy, process governance
Finance/purchase	Planning and controls of costs, budgets, financial forecasts, day-to-day financial processes, contacts negotiations and agreements
Legal	Legal management of contracts, ensuring adherence to regulations and directives, management of IPR
End-users	Users of IT and other business resources who wish to realize business goals and value. These stakeholders demand more from IT than in the past; e.g. Unified Communications And Collaboration (UCAC) and Bring Your Own Device (BYOD)
IT	IT strategy and planning, IT process management, IT service portfolio
Customers	Requirements: Privacy and data protection, user friendly solutions, value-for-money, service support
Partners	Data sharing, information security
Vendors/distributors	Sales of (supporting) solutions
Publishers	Copyright, licensing, IPR

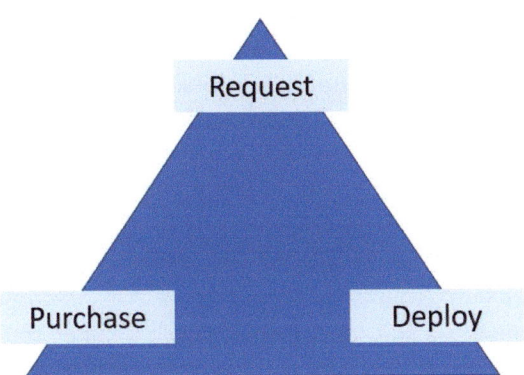

Figure 4. The ITAM 'Bermuda Triangle'

Different instruments can help ITAM to maintain control such as: a predefined IT catalogue, service portfolios, a well-maintained CMDB to ensure new introductions do not negatively affect the existing infrastructure, purchasing policies and procedures, management of licenses, etc.

1.2 STANDARDS AND BEST PRACTICES

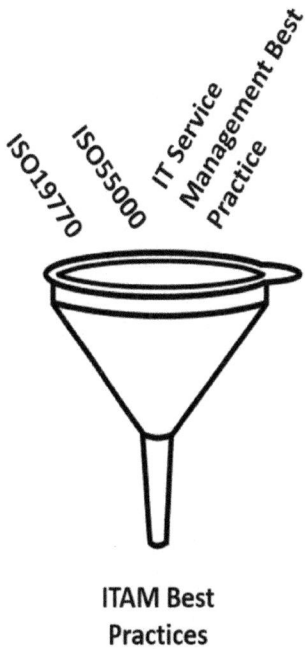

ITAM Best Practices

Figure 5. ITAM best practices

1.2.1 ITAM best practices and related international standards

ISO/IEC 19770 family
Information technology - Software asset management & IT asset management.
Parts of the 19770 family:
- 19770-1: Processes and Tiered Assessment of Conformance; establishes a baseline for an integrated set of processes for Software Asset Management (SAM), divided into tiers to allow for implementing them and achieving recognition.
- 19770-2: Software Identification Tag; establishes specifications for tagging software to optimize its identification and management.
- 19770-3: Software Entitlement Tag; establishes a set of terms and definitions which may be used when discussing software entitlements (an important part of software licenses). It also provides specifications for a transport format which enables the digital encapsulation of software entitlements, including associated metrics and their management.
- 19770-5: Introduction and Vocabulary; provides an overview of the ISO/IEC 19770 family of standards, an introduction to IT asset management (ITAM) and software asset management (SAM), a brief description of the foundation principles and approaches on which SAM is based, and consistent terms and definitions for use throughout the ISO/IEC 19770 family of standards.

Other parts are presently under construction, and ISO.org has also launched a self-assessment tool for software asset management. (Source: ISO.org)

ISO 55000
Asset management - Overview, principles and terminology.
- ISO 55000 is the first set of International Standards for Asset Management.
- Enables an organization to achieve its objectives through an efficient, consistent and sustainable management of its assets.
- Provides an overview of asset management, its principles and terminology, and the expected benefits from adopting asset management.

IT Service Management (ITSM) best practice
ITIL
- The most widely accepted approach to IT service management in the world.
- Provides a cohesive set of best practices, drawn from the public and private sectors internationally.
- Aligns IT services with the needs of business through a set of practices each covering an area of the service management lifecycle.
- Allows the organization to establish a baseline from which it can plan, implement and measure.

ISO/IEC 20000
ITIL is mapped in ISO/IEC 20000. This ISO standard recognizes the way that ITIL can be used to meet the requirements set out for the ISO/IEC 20000 certification and the interdependent nature with ITIL.

In the context of ITAM we can use the following metaphor to describe the relationship between ITAM and ITSM.

IT Asset Management		IT Service Management		
The complete car body is constructed using 'assets' that run through the lifecycle from planning to purchase, running the car all the way up to disposal in accordance with regulations.	+	IT Service management best practices forms the engine that keeps the lifecycle process running. (many cars use engines from another manufacturer).	=	

1.2.2 Requirements for the management of assets
IT assets are highly inter-connected, and their value is realized by their combined performance within complex systems. IT assets require different types of decision making at each different level of management in the organization. Figure 6 shows these different levels of asset management and their requirements.

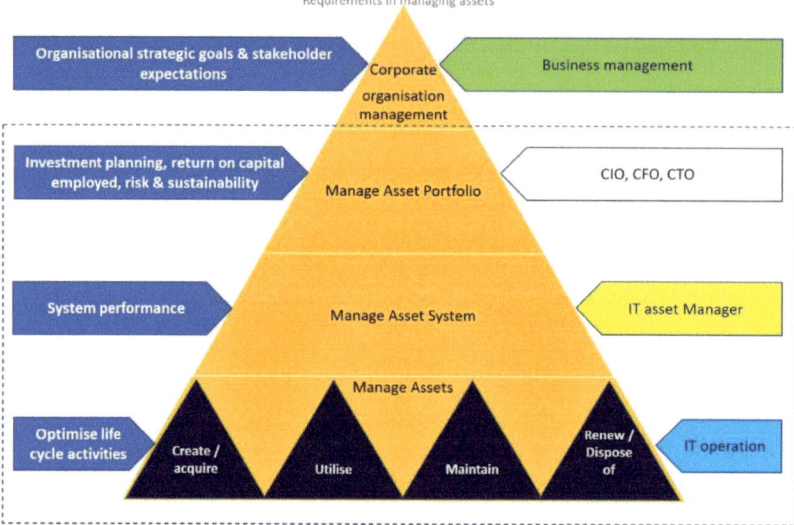

Figure 6. ITAM requirements for the management of assets

An ITAM management system: a basic structure

An ITAM management system needs to be implemented in order to overcome typical hurdles in the organization such as having a short-term vision, budget protectionism, departmental silos with conflicting priorities and firefighting instead of looking for structural improvements. A good ITAM management system enables alignment of business goals with day-to-day operations, culture change, proactive and collaborative behavior. Figure 7 shows the minimum requirements for an ITAM system.

Figure 7. ITAM basic management system

1 Introduction to IT Asset Management (ITAM)

■ 1.3 ITAM MODELS

1.3.1 The ITAM process framework

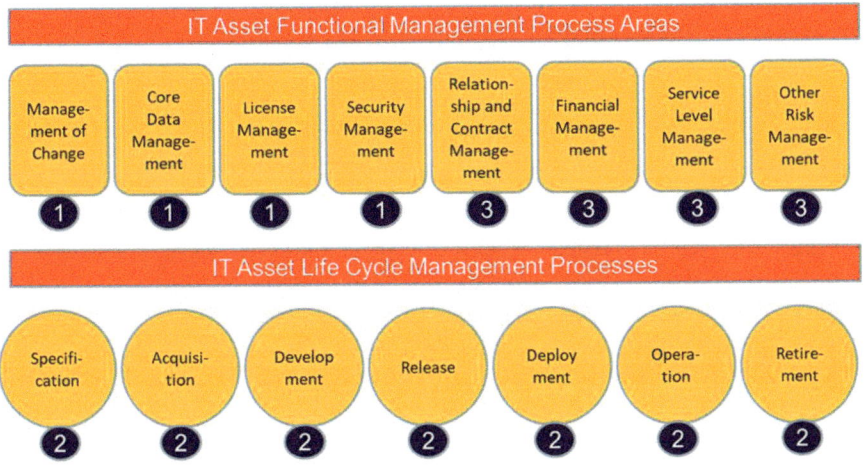

Figure 8. ITAM process framework

Process types are either life cycle or functional. Life cycle management processes are those which reflect stages in the life cycle of the IT assets themselves. Examples are: Acquisition, Release, and Deployment. Functional management processes, in contrast, generally apply across multiple life cycle processes (and hence the term 'cross-cutting' processes is sometimes used). Examples are: Change management, License management, and Relationship and contract management.

1.3.2 Approach to implementing ITAM in practice

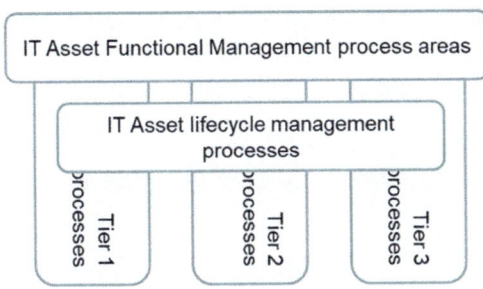

•**Tier 1**: Trustworthy Data. Achieving this tier means knowing what you have so that you can manage it. This includes having reasonable assurance about license compliance.

•**Tier 2**: Life Cycle Integration. Achieving this tier means greater efficiency and cost-effectiveness throughout the IT asset life cycle.

•**Tier 3**: Optimization. Achieving this tier means greater efficiency and effectiveness through focus on cross-cutting functional management process areas.

The ISO 19770-1 approach to implementing ITAM in practice is through a tiered implementation. We will start with the processes defined at the ITAM organizational framework and ITAM Tier framework processes.

After Tier 1 has been implemented then the ITAM organizational framework and ITAM Tier framework processes will be improved and maintained so it fits the tier implementation.

Each Tier has specific processes that are identified as Tier-specific processes. Those processes will be developed in the department and implemented at this specific Tier. Each Tier implementation will have a top down approach.

1.3.3 The importance of conducting a gap analysis

The Gap analysis should be applied before implementing the ITIL/ISO best practices – as a compass pointing the direction to go. The main goal of the gap analysis is to find out which processes are already implemented, and how useful they can be for ITAM. Other goals are to determine the ITAM objectives of the organization, to define a path to reach those organizational objectives and to prioritize ITAM activities and practices.

What is a gap analysis?
- IST: Where are we now?
  - 'Objectives', and which useful processes are already in place?
- SOLL: Where do we want to be?
  - Processes that need implementing and activities that need to be undertaken to reach our objectives.

Actions to be taken after the GAP analysis
- Involve the key roles and ensure commitment (stakeholders?)
  - Communicate the objectives and ITAM practices.
  - Ensure commitment.
- Go 'there' and evaluate (e.g. the Lean activity of 'Gemba walk' which is much like 'Management By Walking Around' (MBWA); an activity that takes management to the front lines).

1 Introduction to IT Asset Management (ITAM)

Exam preparation: Chapter 1

To help prepare for the exam, we have included multiple choice and so-called 'get it' questions (the answer key can be found at the end of this workbook). Additionally, you are provided with an overview of terms you should be familiar with.

Sample exam questions
1. To get success with ITAM some key components are important. Which key components are important?
   A. Make sure all levels of IT assets are managed and controlled.
   B. Have a good relationship with publishers, vendors, customers, legal and finance.
   C. Have a good knowledge and understanding of goals, the motivation and the key drivers from stakeholders across the organization.
   D. Fulfill stakeholder expectations.

2. ISO/IEC 19770 is a standard related to ITAM. What is its purpose?
   A. It is a standard for managing IT assets assisting in managing the risks and minimizing the costs of IT assets.
   B. It is an international standard for People and Information asset management to availability of IT assets.
   C. It is part of best practice guidance within the ITIL framework (Information Technology Infrastructure Library).
   D. It is part of information security management standard (ISO27001) to minimize risks of IT Infrastructure.

3. The CIO/CFO needs to have insight in the IT asset portfolio. Which activities help to get that insight?
   A. The CIO/CFO needs information or needs to be involved about Investment planning and risk & sustainability of IT assets.
   B. Define and continual improvement of the lifecycle and organizational strategic goals.
   C. Insight in the system performance and process control of IT assets.
   D. Utilization of IT assets in the organization.

4. The ITAM process framework is a combination of standards and best practices. Which of the following is most important to enable the ITAM process framework?
   A. Automatic discovery of hardware, database tooling, measure of software utilization.
   B. Risk assessment, business case templates, RACI models.
   C. Request fulfillment of IT asset, automatic deployment of IT assets.
   D. Service management systems, asset discovery, deployment tools.

5. To start up an IT asset management program, the IT Asset Manager needs to have insight. What information from a GAP analysis is useful information for the IT Asset Manager to prepare the IT Asset Management program?
   A. A project initiation documentation (PID) plan for the implementation of IT Asset Management.
   B. A list of KPIs to ensure the success of IT Asset Management.
   C. A list of stakeholders and their key roles.
   D. Processes already in place and which can improve the implementation of an IT Asset Management program.

'Get it' questions

1. Recall the definition of IT Asset Management (ITAM).
Key words: strategic, IT assets, lifecycle, practices.

2. Name at least four objectives of IT Asset Management (ITAM).

3. Name at least four benefits of IT Asset Management (ITAM).

4. Place the different phases of the ITAM lifecycle in their correct order in the lifecycle model.

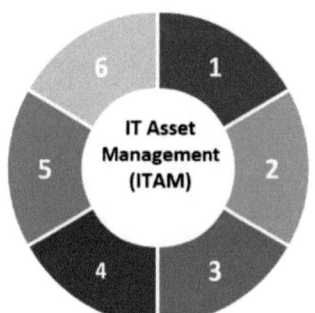

- Receive
- Retire
- Procure
- Request
- Manage
- Strategy/plan

5. a. Explain the so-called 'Bermuda Triangle' of ITAM.
   b. Name some instruments that can help ITAM maintain control over the 'Bermuda Triangle'.

6. Which best practice models and standards help to create the ITAM best practices?

Hardware Asset Management (HAM): Exam requirements

2. Hardware Asset Management (HAM)	20%
2.1 Introduction to HAM	
2.2 Identify and manage hardware assets	
2.3 Best practices, tools and mobile devices	

2 Hardware Asset Management (HAM)

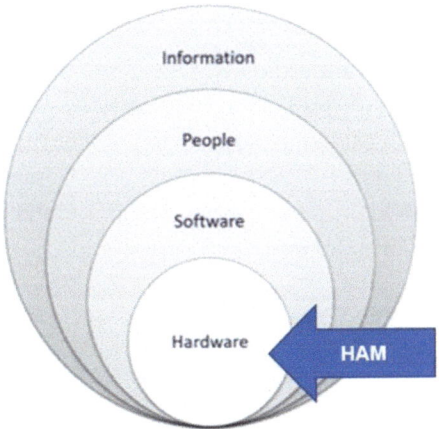

■ 2.1 INTRODUCTION TO HAM

2.1.1 Defining HAM

Hardware Asset Management (HAM) can be defined as the management of the hardware asset portfolio from acquisition through retirement, thus enabling the organization in making business decisions based on meaningful and measurable financial objectives and as a result getting the most value from the hardware assets. A key focus is aligning the organization's hardware asset management strategy with operational goals while offering adequate risk protection.

> **Hardware** refers to the physical components that make up a computer system.
> **Hardware Asset** refers to a managed hardware component.

In 'real life', most organizations know three 'types' of assets: managed assets, unmanaged assets and those in the grey area in between; what about employees bringing their own devices (BYOD)? HAM is tightly connected to SAM as the two asset types cannot be separated.

2.1.2 The purpose and the benefits of HAM
Hardware Asset Management is responsible for the management of the hardware asset portfolio from acquisition through retirement.

Objectives
- Getting the most value from the hardware assets.
- Enabling the organization in making business decisions based on meaningful and measurable financial information and objectives.
- Creating hardware standards and maintain those standards.
- Management of the physical components of computers, mobile devices and networks from acquisition, implementation, process adjustments, deployment to disposal.
- Aligning the organization's hardware asset management strategy with operational goals while offering adequate risk protection: 'a key focus'.

Benefits to different stakeholders
The possible benefits to the different stakeholders are:

IT management: Enabling knowledge-based business decisions with respect to procurement, replacement, disposal and re-use of an asset.

IT operations: Agility – short response time, support the business, re-use of hardware, use of standard hardware services.

Contract and procurement management: Request standard services, easier negotiation – standard hardware services.

Financial management: Cost savings – reduction of over-disposal and over-procurement, compliance foundation data.

Business: Minimize risk of information security, software compliance and data loss.

2.1.3 Overview of the HAM-lifecycle

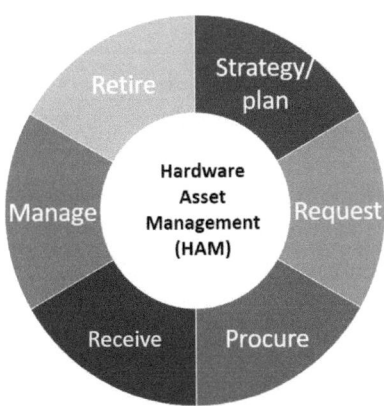

Figure 9. The HAM lifecycle

When initially going through the HAM-lifecycle questions need to be answered, and when the process gets going it is recommended to revisit these questions at a regular interval; this is part of the continuous improvement process. Typical questions to ask at each stage of the lifecycle are:

1. **Strategy / plan:** Which benefits need to be included (managed) and how are we going to manage them? In which way do we document our assets and how do we support management of assets by tools?
2. **Request:** Who requests the asset and for which purpose? Is the procedure part of an existing service level agreement? Is the asset part of the service catalogue?
3. **Procure:** What are the costs of buying and maintaining the asset throughout the lifecycle?
4. **Receive:** When was it received, has it been properly documented? Has it been tested for use?
5. **Manage:** When, and to whom, was the asset deployed? e.g. distribution of 'standard' computer resources, etc. Where is the physical location?
6. **Retire:** Does the asset need to be archived, disposed of or returned to the vendor under the lease contract? Or can it be re-used after refurbishing? What are the regulations for a proper disposal?

■ 2.2 IDENTIFICATION AND MANAGEMENT OF HARDWARE ASSETS

2.2.1 Determining whether an IT hardware asset should be tracked and managed

A rule of thumb is that hardware assets need to be managed if they are of great value, both monetary or to the business, if they are tied to contracts such as lease agreements in which case you do not legally own them, or if they are part of the service value chain and fall under service (level) agreements. Apart from the question of what needs to be tracked you will have to consider how to track them.

The financial terms for leasing of hardware will typically include:
- Total payment per asset in the hardware asset contractual lifecycle
- Maintenance
- Warranty
- Insurance
- Data wiping
- Return cost – Labelling and freight.

Questions: assets are managed in order to know:
- When and from whom was the asset acquired?
- Is it leased or owned by the company?
- What are the costs associated with each asset during its lifecycle?
- Who uses the asset?
- How is it used?
- When has it been deployed?
- Where is it physically located?
- When was it retired and disposed of?

Stakeholders

Figure 10. Hardware Asset Management stakeholders

The prime question with regard to stakeholders is: *'who needs what information about which assets?'* Some examples of the roles and responsibilities of the main stakeholders and their information requirements are listed below.

> **Service desk:** supports the end-user organization. Information about assets (also known as configuration items) is necessary in order to be able to deliver support under the Service Level Agreements (SLA).
>
> **Software Asset Manager:** responsible for all software used 'on the hardware' even if the hardware is not used at that moment in time.
>
> **Hardware Asset Manager:** responsible for all hardware assets and delivery of valid information to contract management, etc.
>
> **Procurement manager:** responsible for the use of mature processes and procedures used for the procurement of hardware assets.
>
> **Contract manager:** responsible for the match of contracts with services.
>
> **System administrators:** work with both hardware and software assets on a daily basis in order to guarantee availability, capacity and security of services.

2.2.2 Examples of hardware standards and considerations when to use them

For each class of users such as end-users, system administrators, mobile users, power users, etc., a standard type of 'computer' can be defined that can meet current and anticipated user needs for several years. Some examples are listed below.
- Laptop standard
- Mobile device standard
- Desktop standard
- Printer standard
- Server standard.

The main benefit of using these standards is that they enable the management of and control over hardware assets. However, they should always cover business needs and must be maintainable. Otherwise the cost will exceed the profit. Computer standards are, amongst other criteria, based on current technology available and the common need of each user class.

Other considerations for their use:
- Cost per asset type – low cost assets will probably not be maintainable.
- Volume of assets in the organization – one plotter versus 1000 laptops.
- Asset lifecycle and depreciation.
- Security risk.
- Legal requirements.
- Asset impact on the productivity.

- Asset redeployment.
- Mobility.
- Business needs per asset type.
- Internal IT Needs per asset type.
- What to put in the Internal and external Service Catalogue.

2.2.3 Disposal standards

The main objectives for proper disposal are protection of intellectual property, ensuring software compliance, privacy and data protection, enabling tracking of assets even after disposal, financial (end-of-life status for tax purposes), proper disposal of electronics and hazardous material, minimize risk when IT assets are disposed and it is done cost-effectively, and finally support and adapt green strategies. Disposal is part of the 'retirement' stage of the HAM lifecycle.

> **Requirements for registration: terminology**
> **Disposal certificate** (not a legal document!)
> Needs at least:
> - Serial number
> - Data of wiping
> - Data wiping method
> - Name of the company
> - LOT number
> - Sanitation standard used
> - Signature.
>
> **A lot number** is an identification number assigned to a particular quantity or lot of material from a single manufacturer.

2.2.4 The HAM lifecycle in an organization

In this section, we will zoom in on the 'Manage' stage of the HAM-lifecycle. Before a hardware asset can be deployed it first needs to be configured; organization-specific parameters and settings, e.g. for the network and security, need to be set. Some server platforms will first receive a virtualization layer before system and/or application software is installed.

During the lifecycle patch and update, it is important to apply a proper management. As end-users, we are accustomed to Windows, Linux or iOS updates. Within a corporate infrastructure these updates need rigorous testing before being distributed because they can have negative impact on organization-specific applications and settings.

Table 2. Concise overview of legislation and standards

Type	Name/Acronym	Description
Acts (USA), Regulations, Directives and Decisions (EU)		
EU Directive	WEEE	**2012/19/EU** of the European Parliament and of the Council of 4 July 2012 on waste of electrical and electronic equipment (WEEE) On 18 April 2017: The Commission adopted the 'WEEE package' including: an implementing regulation (EU law) which will eventually replace this directive.
EU Directive	RoHS	**2011/65/EU** of the European Parliament and of the Council of 8 June 2011 on the restriction of the use of certain hazardous substances in electrical and electronic equipment.
USA Act	RCRA	The Resource Conservation and Recovery Act (RCRA) is the public law that creates the framework for the proper management of hazardous and non-hazardous solid waste.
EU Council Decision	Basel Convention	Convention on the control of transboundary movements of hazardous wastes and their disposal (Basel Convention). 93/98/EEC and 97/640/EC.
Standards		
International standard	ISO 14000	ISO 14000 family - Environmental management systems ■ 14001 - Requirements with guidance for use ■ 14004 - General guidelines on implementation ■ 14005 - Guidelines for the phased implementation of an environmental management system, including the use of environmental performance evaluation ■ 14006 - Guidelines for incorporating eco design.
Certificates		
EPA	R2	Originally developed by the U.S. Environmental Protection Agency (EPA), the R2 Practices standard defines a set of practices for use in the recycling or disposal of used electronic devices, including computers, peripherals, cell phones and televisions.
e-stewards.org	E-stewards	The e-Stewards Standard was created by the environmental organization Basel Action Network in 2009. e-Stewards recyclers are certified through annual audits to the e-Stewards Standard. The e-Stewards Certification is supported by the United States Environmental Protection Agency (EPA).
ISRI.org	RIOS	The Recycling Industry Operating Standard™ (RIOS™) is an integrated quality, environmental, health and safety management system certification.

Because of changes, all documentation needs updating which is one of the tasks of asset management. Specifications of hardware standards may change, users of assets are leaving and new users join the organization, locations change, etc.

Another aspect of the management phase is remote management of mobile assets and BYOD devices.

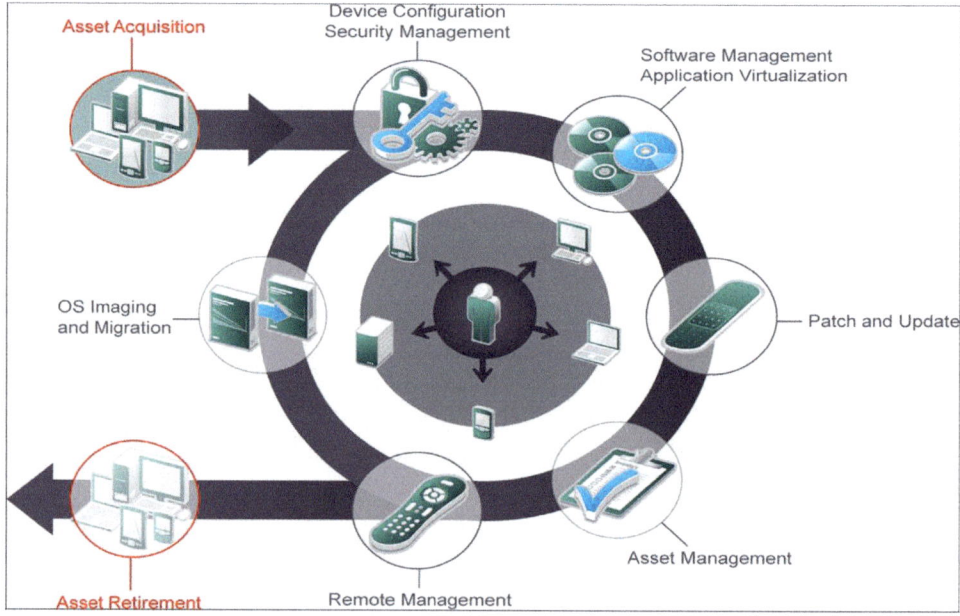

Figure 11. The hardware lifecycle process

During this lifecycle, IT operations will need to receive input from the following stakeholders:
- Contract manager: supplier contracts and terms.
- Security manager: policies, regulations.
- Software Asset Manager: software compliance, terms of use.
- Financial manager: acquisition, disposal, depreciation, hardware forecasts.
- Service desk: request fulfilment, service offerings.

■ 2.3 BEST PRACTICES, TOOLS AND MOBILE DEVICES

2.3.1 Tool considerations for HAM
Reflections
Historically, Hardware Asset Management has been the 'entry level' into IT Asset Management for many corporations. This is primarily due to the fact that HAM is tool-centric and the HAM tool market is quite mature, since a tool will deliver nearly all the information needed in good HAM.

ITAM is data-driven, making the use of the right tool very important, and therefore HAM tool considerations should be ITAM tool considerations. Modern tools are integrated tools for the management of all types of assets, services, documentation such as contracts, associated processes, etc.

Ways of tracking hardware
- Network scanning (IP address, MAC/IMEI)
- RFID scanning
- Tagging barcode / QR code
- Manual registration: e.g. computer hardware inventory form.

Hardware asset record attributes (a type of hardware inventory information)
Attributes describe the characteristics of an asset that are valuable to record and which will support HAM and the other ITSM processes it supports. Some examples are listed below.
- CPU type, CPU speed, CPU count, physical versus logical count.
- Installed physical memory.
- Operating system, edition and service pack.
- Information about extended OS properties including 64-bit, terminal server, Server Core, Hyper-V.
- Virtual machine detection, including a virtual machine platform if available.
- Computer manufacturer and computer model, chassis type (if available).
- BIOS version, serial number (e.g. service tag).

plus
- Registered owner, registered company.
- User Account Control (UAC) level; windows.

The first group of assets typically make up a hardware standard. By defining this group of assets as a standard they only must be registered one time only in the description of the standard and not for each and every asset separately.

2.3.2 Mobile device aspects of HAM
A mobile device is just another term for a computer. With the angle that it is often heavily used privately by the end-user, and sometimes also 'owned' by the end-user (BYOD). Hardware that is not owned by the organization falls outside the scope of Hardware Asset Management. So what do we need to do about BYOD (Bring Your Own Device)? BYOD is more and more becoming a grey area because many of these devices are now running corporate apps, and what if a connection is made between a privately owned smart phone and the company's exchange server?

Since BYODs are not corporately managed, these devices and their 'control' belongs in the 'People and Information Asset Management' category. More on this topic will be discussed in Chapter 5 on People and Information Asset Management (PINAM).

Exam preparation: Chapter 2

To help prepare for the exam, we have included multiple choice and so-called 'get it' questions (the answer key can be found at the end of this workbook). Additionally, you are provided with an overview of terms you should be familiar with.

Sample exam questions
1 The Software Asset Manager is depending on receiving information/data from the Hardware Asset Manager. What information should the Hardware Asset Manager need to deliver to the Software Asset Manager?
   A. A full list of all current processes and procedure used to manage and control IT assets.
   B. A full list of MAC addresses and IP addresses for the related Hardware Assets.
   C. The Hardware Asset Manager needs to deliver trustworthy and reliable data of all IT assets in scope.
   D. A list of all valid sources which are used to manage and control IT assets.

2. To prepare a Hardware Asset Management program, what is one of the first decisions you need to take?
   A. How the IT Hardware Asset must be managed and controlled.
   B. How to setup the request and procurement process to handle all IT assets.
   C. A definition of the security levels for each hardware asset type to be implemented.
   D. A definition and selection of the IT hardware asset types included in the scope.

3. What is the correct sequence of the Hardware Asset Management lifecycle?
   A. Initiation, Design, Build, Migration, Transition, Closing.
   B. Requirements, Design, Implementation, Verification, Maintenance.
   C. Strategy, Design, Transition, Operations, Continual Service Improvement.
   D. Strategy, Request, Procure, Receive, Manage, Retire.

4. A part of the IT Hardware Asset Managers responsibilities is to manage and control IT hardware assets. Which hardware asset could not be tracked and managed by the Hardware Asset Manager and therefore is a potential risk to the organization?
   A. Laptops and printers that are tied to a contract and implemented as part of the operational Infrastructure.
   B. Expensive hardware assets which have been acquired by organization.
   C. Hardware assets that support business processes and enable specific value to the business.
   D. Hardware assets that are not owned by the organization.

5. IT operation is part of the IT Hardware Asset Management lifecycle and therefore needs to get information and feedback. Which stakeholder is most important for IT operation to receive feedback from?
   A. Contract manager, Software Asset Manager, Financial manager, IT manager, Security manager.
   B. Contract manager, Security manager, Software Asset Manager, Financial manager, Service desk.
   C. Financial manager, IT manager, HR Manager, Policy manager, Test manager, Service desk.
   D. Security manager, Software Asset Manager, Service desk, HR Manager, Test manager.

'Get it' questions

1. Recall the definition of Hardware Asset Management (HAM).
Key words: management, portfolio, assets, lifecycle, business decisions, financial objective, value.

2. Name at least four objectives of Hardware Asset Management (HAM).

3. Name at least four benefits of Hardware Asset Management (HAM).

4. Name some benefits of HAM for each of the following stakeholders:
   - IT management
   - IT operation
   - Contract and procurement management
   - Financial management
   - Business.

5. Name some questions that need to be asked for each of the phases of the HAM lifecycle.

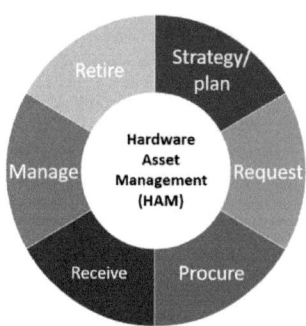

6. By which types of criteria do we determine whether an IT hardware asset should be tracked and managed?

7. a. What is the main benefit of using hardware standards?
   b. Name at least five considerations for their use.

8. What are the main objectives for proper disposal of hardware assets?

9. What are the minimum requirements for a disposal certificate?

10. a. Name the phases of the hardware lifecycle process.
    b. Name some of the stakeholders that need to provide information to IT operations during this lifecycle.
    c. What information is provided by each of these stakeholders?

11. In what ways can HAM track hardware?

12. Explain why Bring Your Own Device (BYOD) is difficult for HAM to manage.

Software Asset Management (SAM): Exam requirements

3. Software Asset Management (SAM)	25 %
3.1 Definition and objectives of SAM	
3.2 The concept of compliance	
3.3 The risks/costs related to software audits	

3 Software Asset Management (SAM)

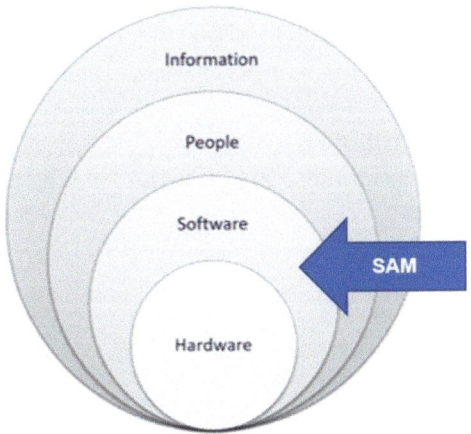

■ 3.1 DEFINITION AND OBJECTIVES OF SAM

3.1.1 Defining SAM

Software Asset Management (SAM) can be defined as a set of best practices managing the complete lifecycle of every software asset, involving cost control, documentation, licensing, redistribution, maintenance etc. SAM is an important part of ITAM and IT Service Management and not optional.

> **Software** is nowadays characterized by a licensed position, and not company owned assets, and tightly connected with the other ITAM areas.
>
> **Software entitlement** is defined in the license agreement with specific terms and conditions.

> A **software license** is a permission to use one or more copies of software bound by a contract. The licensee does not become the owner of the software.
>
> **CAPEX and OPEX**; software assets are business assets and are traditionally viewed as capital expenditures (i.e. given a written off value at the point of purchase). Although new models of deployment (e.g. SaaS) could see this revised as operational expenditures.

Hardware and Software Asset Management are tightly knit together because software runs on hardware, even in a virtual environment, and computer hardware does not do anything without software. SAM is the most crucial ITAM area, representing the greatest financial and legal risk in terms of vendor license conditions and complex compliance regulations.

Software assets composition (examples of attributes)
Software assets can be described by a variety of attributes. The list is not limited to the following examples:
- License information;
- Terms and condition for use;
- Support/service contracts;
- License keys and authorization codes;
- Release documentation and user manuals;
- Distribution copies (images);
- Master copies and media;
- Number of instances installed (as opposed to the number of licenses;
- Etc.

3.1.2 The purpose and benefits of SAM
Objectives
SAM has the main objective of optimizing the complete lifecycle of every software component, involving legal and financial risk reduction and cost control. It is regarded as the most crucial ITAM area, representing the greatest financial and legal risk in relation to vendor license conditions and complex compliance regulations. A second goal is to ensure an up-to-date service portfolio which supports the organization's strategy and planning processes.

Benefits
- Managing risks: financial, legal, reputation, privacy and data protection, disruption of operational processes.
- Cost control and savings: reduction of direct costs and support costs, better purchasing position.

- Obtaining competitive advantage: support of business decisions by providing correct and up-to-date information, faster time-to-market, faster integration of organizational parts (e.g. after a merger).
- Enhancing employee motivation and providing a better workplace environment: prevention of repeated incidents, faster implementation of solutions, better problem management.
- Improved IT operations by providing an improved software portfolio.
- An improved software portfolio supporting the overall business drivers.
- Proactive planning and quality decision making.

Potential problems
- Conflict with a decentralized culture;
- Lack of commitment by senior management;
- Lack of clear responsibility;
- Imbalance between customized and off-the-shelf software perspective;
- Underestimating the effort required to identify installed software;
- Legal requirements;
- Software license variation;
- Lack of communication;
- Inability to utilize existing SAM tools.

3.1.3 Overview of the SAM-lifecycle

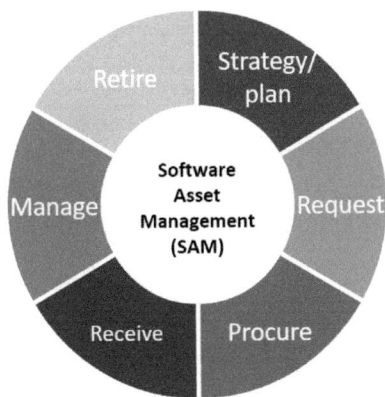

Throughout the SAM-lifecycle there needs to be focus on strategic planning, decision support, cost effectiveness, risk reduction and, last but not least, customer satisfaction.

3.1.4 SAM roles and responsibilities

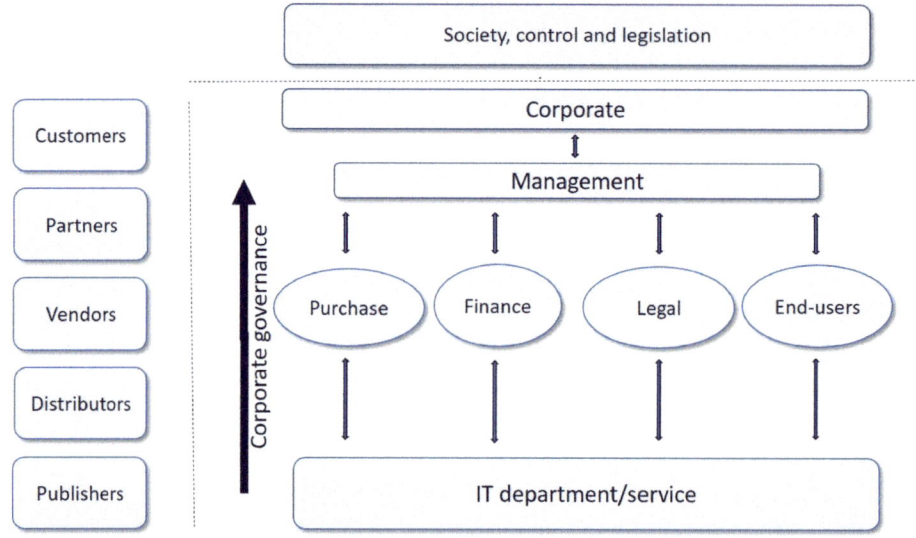

Figure 12. SAM stakeholder map

Internal stakeholders
- Corporate/board of directors: own the SAM vision and strategy, ensuring that strategy is executed at all levels. Senior sponsorship of SAM including policies.
- Management: responsible for defining SAM objectives, roles and responsibilities, and processes and procedures.
- Purchase and finance: procurement and contract management.
- Legal: supports the SAM manager in ensuring compliance.
- End-users: requestors and users of software assets.
- IT department/service organization: management and support of the software asset portfolio.

External stakeholders
- Society: legislation, regulations (i.e. with regard to copyrights, privacy and data protection).
- Customers: have external access to IT systems.
- Partners: exchange of data involves copyright and license issues, data protection and privacy issues (e.g. external data processing).
- Vendors/distributors/resellers: financial and contractual obligations.
- Publishers: exchange of data impacts IPR, compliance.

Internal SAM roles

Software Asset Manager: responsible for the management (tracking & controlling) of all software assets during their lifecycle.

Application manager: responsible for application support and maintenance (including modifications) in cooperation with the vendor. This includes a role in the IT Service Management processes, especially problem management, change management and release management.

SAM tool administrator: manages the tools that support the SAM processes and activities.

Project manager: manages SAM-related projects.

Software & license analyst: responsible for tracking and control of licenses.

Audit manager: quality control and assurance, internal audit, reporting to management and corporate of audit-related information, cooperates with external auditors, creating awareness and ongoing education of staff.

Software deployment manager: specialist deployment role in large organizations.

Table 3. Internal stakeholders needed to support a successful SAM program

Stakeholder	area	results	SAM
HAM	Hardware data	**Compliance:** licensing, security, policy and procedure	Reporting & documentation
Contract/legal	Terms & conditions	Agility	
Procurement	Procurement data	Compliance, faster software delivery	
Management	Policies, rules of conduct	Support, workflow and clear responsibilities	

3.1.5 Introducing SAM best practices

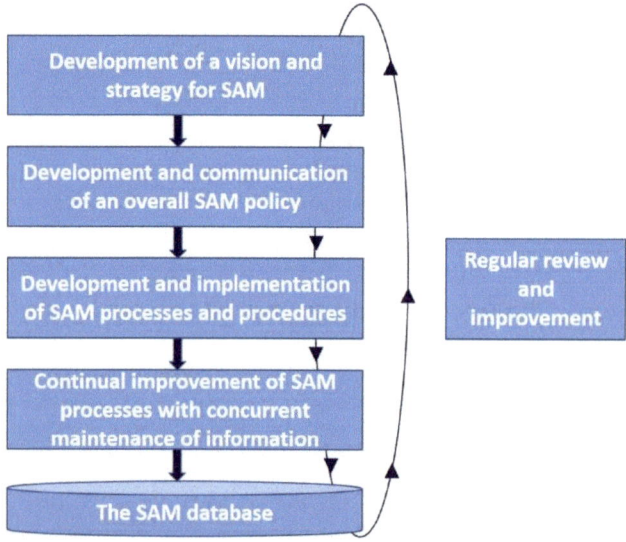

Figure 13. SAM implementation roadmap

SAM implementation roadmap
For each of the phases of the implementation roadmap, examples of considerations for this phase are given below.

PLAN
1. **Development of a vision and strategy for SAM:** gain approval for a SAM program from as high up in the organization as possible, have documented goals and objectives.

DO
2. **Development and communication of an overall SAM policy:** ensure that all personnel are fully aware of what is expected of them.
3. **Development and implementation of SAM processes and procedures:** understand how you are going to capture inventory data, and what is involved in comparing that to licensing data, and with regard to tool selection. Ensure that your organization fully understands the business requirements that shape the criteria you use to select the software to support your SAM program. Consider what documentation is needed to manage the lifecycle of software through your organization, and the interaction of those policies and procedures with your SAM program.

CHECK & ACT

4. **Continuous improvement of SAM processes with concurrent maintenance of information:** benchmark your existing operations so that you can build on the good work already in place, conduct regular process reviews, learn from corrective actions, check for changes in the vision and strategy, plan improvements.

Implementing the SAM process framework

A tiered approach for the implementation of SAM was adopted from ISO/IEC 19770-1. Each tier has specific processes. See figure 14.

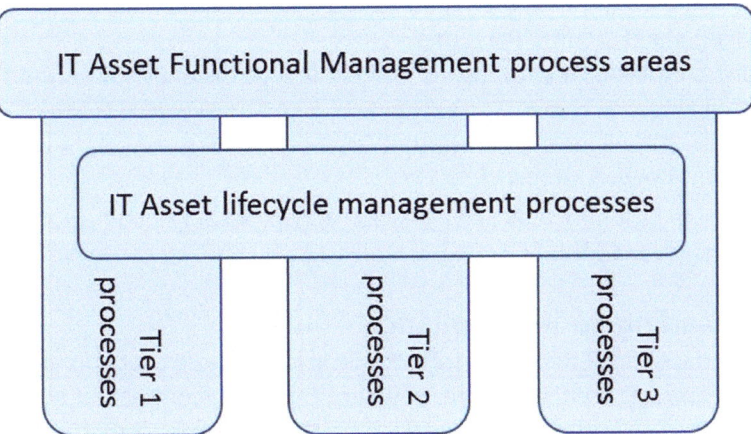

Figure 14. SAM tiered approach

The total approach is top-down. Each tier brings specific benefits to the organization, and can be summarized as follows:

- Tier 1: Trustworthy data. Achieving this tier means knowing what you have so that you can manage it. This includes having reasonable assurance about license compliance.
- Tier 2: Life cycle integration. Achieving this tier means greater efficiency and cost-effectiveness throughout the IT asset life cycle.
- Tier 3: Optimization. Achieving this tier means greater efficiency and effectiveness through focus on cross-cutting functional management process areas.

3.2 THE CONCEPT OF COMPLIANCE

> Compliance can be defined as "conformity in fulfilling official requirements" (e.g. laws, regulations, the requirements of a standard, contractual clauses, etc.).
>
> *Source of the definition: Merriam-Webster*

Compliance (types)
- Licensing compliance: Ensuring that the use of all software within the organization remains within all legal and contractual terms.
- Security compliance: Ensuring that software policies are consistent with security policies and plans.
- Policy and procedure compliance: Ensuring that SAM policies are consistent with corporate policies, strategies and plans.
- Standards compliance: Ensuring that SAM policies and procedures comply with adopted standards such as CMM, COBIT.

3.2.1 Violations leading to incompliancy

Most organizations find it difficult to control software licenses because every provider uses its own type of contract, license scheme, payment methods, contractual terms and conditions, terminology, update strategy, etc. Traditionally, large organizations bought corporate or enterprise licenses paying the same amount of license fee irrespective of the number of users and the level of use per user. Present day Cloud SaaS services mostly use a pay-per-use scheme which can save money in contrast with corporate 'bulk' contracts.

Examples of violations of license terms
- Software being used without licenses being purchased or loss of proof of license:

Violations of license terms	Examples of controls
Software is sometimes installed without going through the complete procurement process or renewal of the authorization (i.e. re-use).	Only allow software installations by centralized software deployment and controlled by software asset management. Exceptions should be reported to software asset management, including the underpinning license proof (preferably controlled by a software metering process).
Proof of purchased licenses may be lost or proof is not official because of purchases from a reseller or after an upgrade of the software.	Proposed counter measure: centralized software procurement controlled by software asset management.

Lack of understanding of licensing terms and conditions.	Introduce Software License Management as a sub task of Software Asset Management, if necessary provided/supported by a specialized vendor.
Lack of records about software usage and often not even the number of PCs in use.	Establish software metering for hardware and software inventory and software usage metering to enable license utilization.

- Incorrect reliance on resellers:

Violations of license terms	**Examples of controls**
Purchase from or installation by suppliers of unlicensed or counterfeit software.	Only use a certified software license reseller.
Lack of proof of license.	Establish software license management and perform regular (at least yearly) audits to demonstrate compliancy.
Pirated software: acts of 'piracy' may be involved such as OEM un-bounding, soft-lifting, hard disk loading, etc.	Only allow software installations by centralized software deployment and controlled by software asset management.

3.2.2 Types of software compliance

Software licenses provide the right to use software, but this is totally separate from the legal rights to the software itself. This legal right is normally kept by the software manufacturer or other third party. Licenses may be bought or may be 'free' subject to special terms and conditions. Even 'open source' software normally has a license even though payment may not be required.

■ 3.3 THE RISKS AND COSTS RELATED TO SOFTWARE AUDITS

3.3.1 Defining audit

Software audit can be defined as a review of software assets conducted either internally or by an external compliance agency or software publisher to confirm compliance to copyright.

During an audit a lot of detailed information in the fields of existence of processes, procedures, documentation and proof of compliance (do we live by the rules?) needs to be provided to the auditor(s). Examples are:
- Hardware and software inventory information.
- Purchasing policies, procedures, records and all related documentation.
- Software usage in relation to licenses and all license information.
- End-user policies.
- Description of asset-standards, such as software images and their deployment.
- Vendor/reseller documentation, such as contracts and invoices.

3.3.2 Possible ramifications of an audit
The consequence of a violation or an audit could be:
- Reputational damage: your organization can be 'named and shamed'.
- Security violations: illegal and counterfeit software may cause virus infections, or breaches of personal data may be discovered.
- Down time: a vendor may seize your software assets as part of a court case over a license dispute
- Delivery up: delivery up is a legal term for "the act of giving something back to someone, especially so that it can be destroyed. Examples include goods produced in breach of intellectual property." (Source: translegal.com).
- Administrative and/or monetary fines: under EU law fines for repetitive damaging breaches of personal data can be punished by monetary fines up to 20,000,000 EUR or up to 4% of the annual worldwide turnover of the preceding financial year in case of an enterprise, whichever is greater. (Source: GDPR Article 83, Paragraph 5 & 6).
- Imprisonment: 'worst case scenario'!

Exam preparation: Chapter 3

To help prepare for the exam, we have included multiple choice and so-called 'get it' questions (the answer key can be found at the end of this workbook). Additionally, you are provided with an overview of terms you should be familiar with.

Sample exam questions

1. Software consists of two essential things, the actual software (functionality) and the entitlements. What does an entitlement describe?
   A. How software can be distributed.
   B. The functionality of the software.
   C. How software must be purchased and terms of payment.
   D. The terms and conditions of using the software.

2. What is the purpose of Software Asset Management?
   A. To prevent personnel to use their own devices to run business software.
   B. To avoid or reduce risk, ensure compliance, and control software costs.
   C. To ensure that software is legally obtained.
   D. To ensure strategic planning and forecasting of software to fulfill the business needs.

3. When software must be upgraded, this could be a challenge for the IT Software Asset Manager. Which is the most significant challenge?
   A. The specifications and documentation of hardware are not sufficient.
   B. Inflexible and immature installation processes.
   C. The proof of purchase of the software is not documented.
   D. End-users are not educated to use the functionality of the software.

4. A SAM program often fails because of what?
   A. Roles and responsibilities are not clear.
   B. Software cannot be maintained and upgraded.
   C. The software portfolio is outsourced.
   D. Inflexible and immature internal policies.

5. The software publisher (copyright holder) has any right to initiate an audit. What is the purpose of an external software audit?
   A. To verify that the software in use is at the correct version and is aligned with the purpose in the contract.
   B. To verify that the software is used correctly and compliant to the terms and conditions and that licenses have been paid.

C. To verify that the software being used is in compliance with the general software policies in the organization.
D. To make sure that software is balanced in relation to the number of licenses purchased.

'Get it' questions

1. Recall the definition of Software Asset Management (SAM).
Key words: best practice, software asset, lifecycle, cost control, maintenance, licensing, distribution, documentation.

2. Name at least four objectives of Software Asset Management (SAM).

3. Name at least four benefits of Software Asset Management (SAM).

4. Name at least four attributes that make up a software asset.

5. Name at least three different stakeholders belonging to the two categories of stakeholders in the SAM stakeholder map:
   1. Internal stakeholders
   2. External stakeholders.

6. Name at least five internal SAM roles and their responsibilities.

7. What are the stages of the SAM implementation roadmap?

8. Name the main characteristic of each of the four process tiers in the SAM framework.

9. Name three types of compliance that are specifically important for SAM.

10. Explain how Software is sometimes used without licenses being purchased, or proof of license has been lost.

11. Give some examples of information that needs to be provided to the auditor(s) of a software audit.

12. Name a few possible consequences that may be brought up by an external audit.

Services and Cloud Asset Management (SEAM): Exam requirements

4. Services and Cloud Asset Management (SEAM)	20 %
4.1 Definition and objectives of SEAM	
4.2 The concept of Services and cloud	
4.3 The practice of SEAM	
4.4 Contracts and contract negotiation in SEAM	

4 Services and Cloud Asset Management (SEAM)

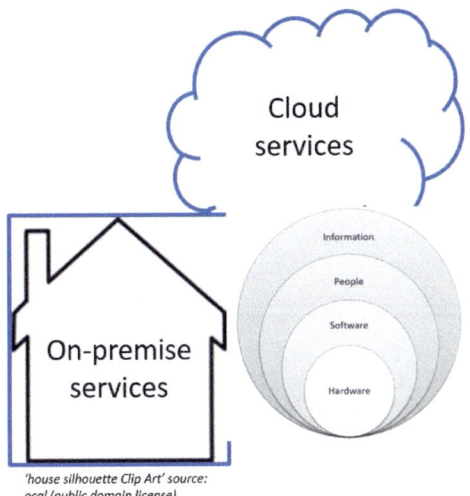

'house silhouette Clip Art' source:
ocal (public domain license)

■ 4.1 DEFINITION AND OBJECTIVES OF SEAM

4.1.1 Defining SEAM

Services and Cloud Asset Management (SEAM) can be defined as the management of multiple platforms across physical, virtual and cloud environments with respect to the organizational needs in terms of storage, data protection, policies and availability.

Cloud services are services delivered from a provider's data center via the Internet. Cloud services are off-premise services as opposed to on-premise (also known as in-house) services. They typically include data storage, backup solutions, web-based application services (apps), application hosting, including licenses, and virtual server platforms. Instead of buying hardware and software to combine into services, cloud computing services are rented or leased, or bought-in through a pay-per-use scheme.

Contract negotiations

Contract negotiations are a key link in the chain of SEAM successes. Therefore it needs to be set up like a proper process. Activities include: need analysis and definition (including a gap analysis), negotiating, measuring the services after delivery, ensuring compliance and continuous improvement of the process.

A good SEAM success rate in cloud contract negotiations is determined by proper and measurable contract clauses such as: services agenda, Agreement terms and conditions and support (e.g. user support, second-level support).

4.1.2 The purpose and benefits of SEAM

The objective of SEAM is to optimize and document the complete lifecycle of every Cloud and service component, including the contractual terms, deliverance and service components with focus on risk reduction and cost control.

> **The following assets should be managed in a Services and cloud solution:**
> - Internal system performances and services
> - Data integration, usability
> - Measurements (SLAs)
> - Contracts ('plural').

General benefits
- The service provider supplies the required services (hardware and/or software) which leads to the optimal use of the company's own IT resources.
- Other benefits include more focus on core business processes, access to complex IT solutions without having to buy them upfront, system capacity and availability can be better matched to actual demand and against lower cost, services are scalable to meet demand at peak times, access to services can be realized at any time, in any place and on any device potentially making the business more agile.

Benefits of Services and Cloud Asset Management (SEAM) related to managing risks
- Gaining control.
- Ensuring a contract and solution that supports the long-term planning in the business.
- Lowering operational costs.
- Avoiding unexpected costs due to tight contract terms.
- Compliance (software, company policies, legal).
- Increased performance in-house and out-of-house.
- Ensuring that the out-of-house architecture enhances the workflow in the organization.

4.2 THE CONCEPT OF SERVICES AND CLOUD COMPUTING

4.2.1 Services and cloud concept

Services and cloud (also known as cloud computing) refers to services delivered from a cloud service provider's server, and includes online data storage, backup solutions, web-based services, hosted applications, database processing, etc. Cloud computing is a modern form of application hosting 'over the Internet'. Cloud services are generally described as 'anything as a Service or XaaS. The most prominent variety is called Software as a Service (SaaS). SaaS can be categorized as 'out-of-house' services as opposed to services from the company's own servers: 'in-house' also known as 'on-premise'.

> *So it is just another word for outsourcing!?*

End users and private users of Internet are often not aware that they are using services from the cloud. But where would they be without Dropbox, Facebook, LinkedIn, Spotify, etc., etc.? All these are examples of cloud services.

The three main cloud service models are:

> **PaaS** – Platform as a service: networks, running servers, storage and tools from the cloud on which a customer can develop, test and run his own applications.
>
> **IaaS** – Infrastructure as a service: data center infrastructure on demand. Saves customers capital expenditure because of the pay-per-use model.
>
> **SaaS** – Software as a service: running software from the cloud including licenses, maintenance (i.e. updates) and support. Potential money saver because of pay-per-use. No unused concurrent licenses are needed.

And of course XaaS – 'Anything' as a service; there are now many variations to the theme available such as Security as a Service (SECaaS) and Desktop as a Service.

Moving from in-house services to external SaaS services can bring many advantages for an organization. Cloud service providers sell 'pay-per-use', 'software license included for any period of usage only', no capital expenditure for hardware (i.e. server platforms and storage) for the customer, etc. However, it is easy to ride on a pink cloud and underestimate the actual costs. Actual costs and financial savings will have to be determined before moving into 'the cloud'.

4.2.2 The benefits and pitfalls of Services and cloud computing

Organizational benefits
- Enables the organization to focus on the core business.
- Gives access to complex IT systems without the costs for buying and managing the underlying software and hardware.
- Required system performances and at the same time lower operational costs.
- Scalability of server requirements, the set-up can be adjusted immediately when the needs of the organization change.
- Agility, access to systems and data from various locations, platforms and devices as well as flexible and agile solutions set-up enabling a faster time-to-market and quick service changes.

Possible organizational problems
- Standard solution is not adjusted to the specific needs of the organization.
- Complex compliance positions such as those that are related to international (i.e. EU) or national regulations and laws or standards for data security.
- Geographical location of data storage: many national banking regulations prohibit the storage of banking-related information outside the national borders.
- Privacy and data protection: the new EU General Data Protection Regulation (GDPR) that becomes effective in early 2018 dictates strict rules on movement of privacy-related data outside the EU area.
- Loss of control on: compliance, version updates and influence.
- Lack of transparency.
- Changes in well-known existing IT interfaces and functionality, impact on productivity and workflow, etc.
- Service provider may change your services beyond your request.
- Vendor lock-in.
- Named user accounts may increase license costs (not every user is using the same application at the same time, therefore you typically need less licenses than there are users).

Possible compliance issues
- The cloud provider lets more concurrent users use an application than there are actual licenses.
- Unclear license terms and conditions.
- No logging and reporting of software usage.
- May rely on another layer of resellers.

4.3 THE PRACTICE OF SEAM

4.3.1 Defining SEAM

- SEAM is the management of the multiple platforms across physical, virtual and cloud environments with respect to the organizational needs in terms of storage, data protection, policies and availability. This management of multiple platforms across physical, virtual and cloud environments is called the 'Triple Play' of SEAM.

Services and cloud refers to services delivered from the server of a cloud service provider, and includes online data storage, backup solutions, web-based services, hosted applications, database processing, etc. The service provider supplies the required services (hardware and/or software) which leads to the optimal use of the company's own IT resources.

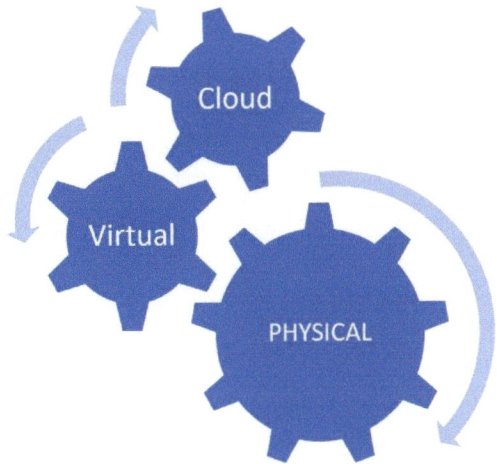

Figure 15. SEAM 'Triple Play'

Overview of the SEAM lifecycle
The SEAM lifecycle looks very much like any outsourcing model. See figure 16. Services and cloud is in fact just a type of outsourcing. The business requires direct services such as Service desk support, user training and alignment of these services with the company policies and goals. Services are delivered by the IT organization, and in this model just a small part of the infrastructure required is on-premise.

4.3.2 The activities of SEAM
SEAM processes and activities include two major areas:
1. Contract negotiations and signing.
2. Operational and practical activities after contract signing.

Pre-negotiating activities are discussed in Section 4.4.1.

Figure 16. SEAM lifecycle

1. Contract negotiations and signing

Contract negotiations and signing are based on a prior analysis of the organization's needs in terms of system characteristics (e.g. performances, storage, agility, scalability, user rights, data movements, usability, support, training, contract management regulations, etc.), service agenda and Agreement terms and conditions.

Tasks
- Definition of terms and SLAs.
- Measurements (SLAs) of delivered services.
- Ensuring that all legal regulations are followed, including license and compliance terms.
- Alignment of the services and the organization needs in terms of storage, data protection, system capability, policies and availability.

Typically, a SEAM manager is also involved in budget planning, strategy planning and contract negotiations to ensure alignment throughout the organization.

2. The operational and practical level & best practices after contract signing

Definition of the activities and measuring points are needed both externally and internally, ensuring that the contractual terms are achieved and the SLAs are met, and that internal compliance is ensured via ongoing processes.

Tasks
- 'One time' task: Internal workflow - clear definition of roles and responsibilities working within the contract governance.
- Routine task: Monitoring of SLAs: service availability, both externally and internally, compliance management and ensuring data connections and a high-level user interface.
- Strategic task: Ongoing attention to required adjustments in the service each time the organization needs change.

> **SAM practices for SEAM environments**
> SAM best practices are required for SEAM, and need to be implemented on at least Tier 1 maturity:
> - Asset identification, verification and inventory management.
> - Licensing compliance and conformance verification.

■ 4.4 CONTRACTS AND CONTRACT NEGOTIATION IN SEAM

4.4.1 Pre-negotiation activities

Contract negotiations need to be properly prepared, and therefore the SEAM contract negotiating process requires a pre-analysis activity or even sub-process.

Pre-analysis before negotiating: some questions to be answered:
- In which areas does our company get added value by this service?
- What are the financial savings and costs in this solution?
- What risks are implied? How can we manage these?
- Any regulations from society that need to be considered?
- Do we have the competencies to negotiate a long-term contract?
- Do we have the resources to manage the contract and to ensure that the contract terms are followed and the SLAs are met?
- How do we plan the change?

Gap Analysis: 'A tool in the pre-signing process'
- What are our IT needs today and in the future? Performance, software, speed time, flexibility, user rights, inventory information, etc.
- How do we plan the journey/migration into the cloud?
- How will it impact the users?
- What activities and resources do we need to get there?
- When migrated, which practices do we need to maintain the standards and objectives?

Role of the SEAM manager
The SEAM manager needs to understand both the business and the vendor, see figure 17.

The SEAM manager needs to understand both the business and the Vendor

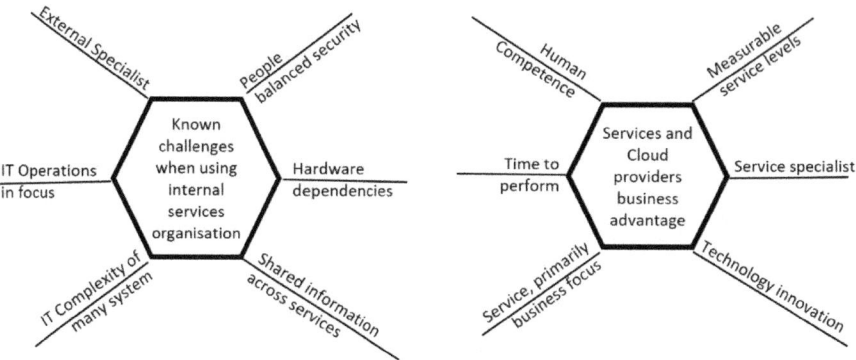

Figure 17. SEAM and the worlds of the internal and external IT provider

4.4.2 Contract clauses and their pitfalls

To prevent SEAM from 'falling into contract clause pits', contracts need to be set up in a proper way. This includes three major areas:

Services agenda
Clear SLAs, including data and server delivery terms.
Clearly defined data ownership.
User rights and traceability.
Access from multiple platforms.
Agreement terms and condition
Clear exit clauses - terms to exit the contract and how to get your data.
Launch of payments - payment starts upon roll-out and not before!
Pricing, a fixed price model, including support and access from different regions and platforms and meaningful regulations for e.g. price increases.
Penalties: services breaches from the provider are tied to financial credits.
Inventory information, the provider should share all inventory data and have clear agreements.
Support
End user support in native language.
Second level complies with enterprise support time.
Training and education program.

4 Services and Cloud Asset Management (SEAM)

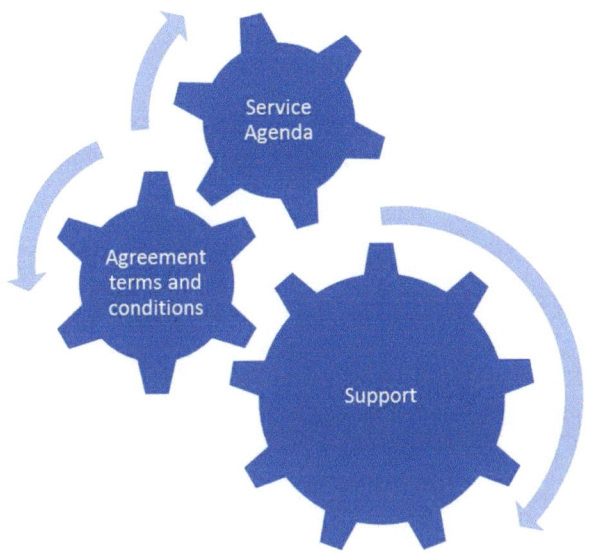

Exam preparation: Chapter 4

To help prepare for the exam, we have included multiple choice and so-called 'get it' questions (the answer key can be found at the end of this workbook). Additionally, you are provided with an overview of terms you should be familiar with.

Sample exam questions
1. Which one is part of the Agreement terms and conditions?
   A. Clear exit clauses.
   B. User rights and traceability.
   C. Clear SLAs, including data and server delivery terms.
   D. Training and education program.

2. Cloud service has a number of benefits. What are the most important benefits from this?
   A. To share servers with other clients is a cheaper solution compared to owning the servers.
   B. Better security and scalability.
   C. Capacity on demand and higher availability of the services.
   D. Agility and scalability of the solution.

3. What is the definition of a Platform as a Service (PaaS) and what does the cloud provider include?
   A. Network, servers, storage & databases.
   B. Computers, virtual machines, databases & firewalls.
   C. Network, servers, storage & tools.
   D. Network, computer, firewalls & virtual machines.

4. Before negotiating the contract, which of the following should be included in the pre-analysis ahead of the negotiation?
   A. A project plan for the journey/migration into the cloud.
   B. A plan of practices for maintaining the standards and objectives.
   C. Establishing in which areas the business gets added value by moving to cloud services.
   D. A plan for how the business will be impacted in the future by performance, software, speed time, flexibility, user rights, inventory information, etc.

5. What is not a possible organizational problem of cloud services?
   A. Standard solution did not adjust to the specific needs of the organization.
   B. Geographical location of data storage.
   C. Enables the organization to focus on the core business.
   D. Service provider may change your services beyond your request.

'Get it' questions

1. Recall the definition of Services and Cloud Asset Management (SEAM).
Key words: multiple platforms, environments: cloud, virtual, physical, organizational needs, policies, storage, availability, privacy, data protection.

2. Name at least four objectives of Services and Cloud Asset Management (SEAM).

3. Name at least four benefits of Services and Cloud Asset Management (SEAM).

4. Describe the concept of Services and cloud.

5. Name and describe the three main cloud service models.

6. What are possible compliance issues for SEAM when using cloud services?

7. Describe the 'Triple Play' of SEAM.

8. a. What are the two major areas of SEAM processes and activities?
   b. Name at least two tasks for each of these two areas.

9. Describe some of the questions for the pre-negotiating activity 'pre-analysis'.

People and Information Asset Management (PINAM): Exam requirements

5. People and Information Asset Management (PINAM)	20 %
5.1 Definition and objectives of PINAM	
5.2 The guiding principles of PINAM	
5.3 The practice of PINAM	
5.4 Services and cloud: BYOD (Bring Your Own Device)	

5 People and Information Asset Management (PINAM)

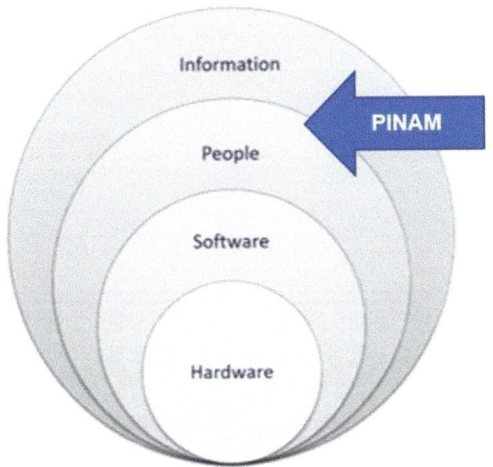

■ 5.1 DEFINITION AND OBJECTIVES OF PINAM

5.1.1 Defining PINAM

People and Information Asset Management (PINAM) can be defined as the management of the complete lifecycle of every valuable information component and the people around it. This involves optimal knowledge sharing and delivery of information to the right people at the right time, control of data security and user rights, data traceability, information transparency, policy setting and enforcement.

People and Information Asset Management (PINAM) regards both people and information (data) as the core assets for an organization. Knowledge, skills and information are indispensable for an organization. Hardware and software can generally be replaced, replacing experienced people is often much more difficult. The management of People and Information refers to data security, access policies and best practices with regard to knowledge and information sharing.

Figure 18 depicts the relationships between the ITAM areas PINAM, SAM, HAM and SEAM.

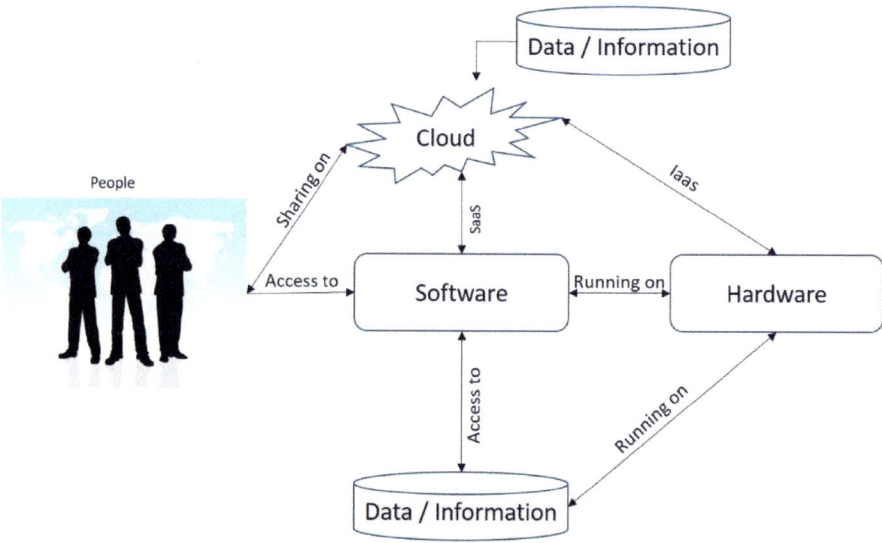

Figure 18. PINAM and the other ITAM areas

> **Data** can be defined as "factual information (as measurements or statistics) used as a basis for reasoning, discussion, decision making or calculation".
>
> **Information** can be defined as "knowledge obtained from investigation, study, or instruction".
>
> *Source: Merriam-Webster*

In fact, information is data that conforms with certain quality criteria making it useful for the organization. Typical criteria are: accurate, specific, timely and organized for a specific purpose such as those mentioned in the definition: instruction, study, decision making, etc.

5.1.2 The purpose and benefits of PINAM

PINAM is responsible for the management of the complete lifecycle of every valuable information component and people. This includes:
- Creating awareness of the risk associated with loss of data.
- Increasing the business value of data and information for the right people at the right time.
- Ensuring an agile and safe workflow and knowledge sharing.
- Ensuring traceability of information

And (a key point):
- Creating a balance between *information agility* and *information security*.

Organizational benefits
- Optimal information and knowledge sharing across desktop and mobile.
- Enhanced company productivity and competitiveness.
- Organizational awareness of the value of corporate information and appropriate handling of this.
- Data/information control, including mobile content.
- Risk reduction.
- Avoiding exposure of valuable company information.
- Avoiding leaks/stopping leaks swiftly.

■ 5.2 THE GUIDING PRINCIPLES OF PINAM

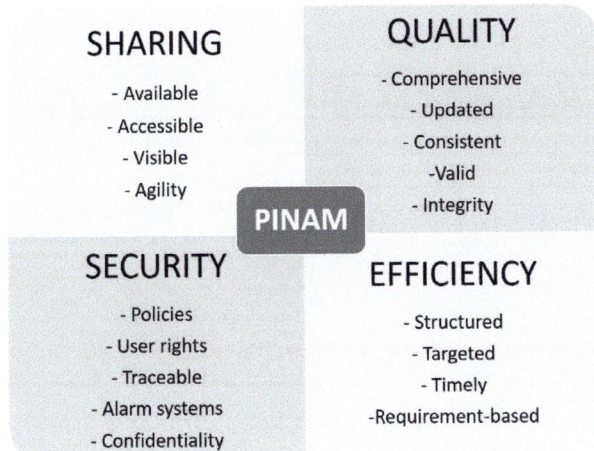

Figure 19. PINAM areas for attention

Legend:

Sharing	Sharing information to support the workflow and productivity.
Quality	Ensuring a high quality of information and data.
Efficiency	Ensuring that information is easy to save and find (structured storing of information).
Security	Ensuring that the right people have access to the right data, including traceability: You need to know where the corporate information is, who uses it, where and with which purpose.

5.2.1 The guiding principles of PINAM

Guiding principles
Information assets are corporate assets.
Availability: information must be available, to the right people at the right time to support the workflow productivity.
Accessibility: information can be accessed anywhere, at any time and from any device
Valuable information needs to be identified, managed and retained corporately.
Visibility: all valuable information should be traceable.
Information Asset Management is a corporate responsibility that needs to be addressed across all functions and levels in an organization.

5.2.2 Principles that support productivity

Principles supporting productivity
Access anywhere: Sharing and managing files from any device.
Rich platform for work: Ensuring the ability to interact with any relevant document through tasks, comments, rich preview and clear permissions.
Cohesive collaboration: Tightly integrated with everyone's preferred mobile and desktop productivity tools.

Restrictions
- **Security:** Centralize content into a secure content platform that integrates identity, device and application management toolsets.
- **Visibility:** Monitor, measure and report on content as it flows to mobile devices and across to customers, partners and vendors.
- **Control:** Control device access, sanction productivity apps, and directly manage how everyone in your organization accesses and uses information.

5.3 THE PRACTICE OF PINAM

5.3.1 PINAM processes and activities

At the present day, most productive employees have three demands to drive their productivity, namely access to information, flexibility in access (at any time and any place), and access even on their own computer devices (BYOD). PINAM is therefore all about the management of important information. The PINAM processes and activities can be divided into four main steps:

1. Information categorization versus content restrictions.
2. Data tagging and user rights management.
3. Data traceability.
4. Policies.

Step 1: Information categorization and content restrictions

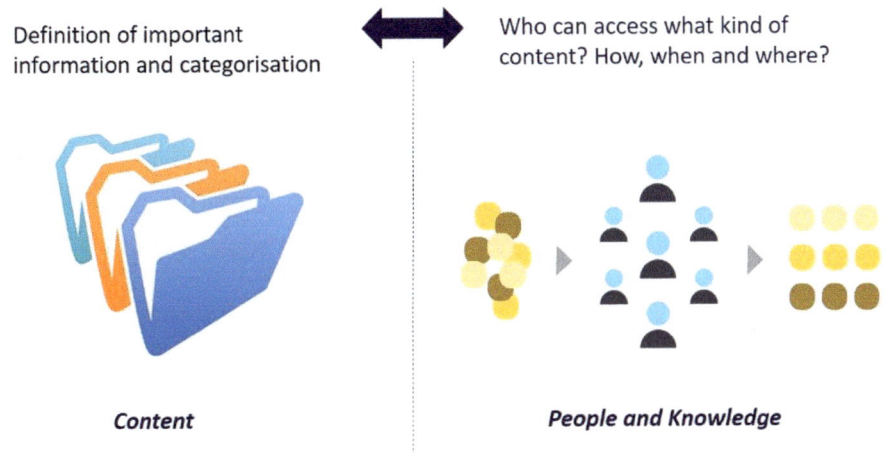

Definition of important information and categorisation ⟷ Who can access what kind of content? How, when and where?

Content — *People and Knowledge*

Restrictions
- Who can access?
- Who can read, edit, etc.?
- Allowed reading time?
- Allowed editing?
- Allowed copying and attaching?
- Allowed forwarding?
- Etc.

Step 2: Data tagging and user rights management

Tagging and management of user rights is addressed on two levels:
- Level 1: (manual)
  - Categorization of data: each category gets its own folder.
  - Restrict access to specific people/groups.
  - ... needs policies...
- Level 2: (automatic)
  - Tagging is done by technology.
  - Only when someone tries to access information, user rights are activated.
  - Processes are logged to ensure consistency.

Step 3: Data traceability
- Traceability is facilitated by **tagging and management of user rights:** Who reads the important information? When? To whom is it shared?
- Traceability also **enables alarm systems**, e.g.: when large amounts of information is copied or shared, or if user patterns vary from normal.

Step 4: Policies
PINAM policies relate to:
- Code of conduct in handling company information.
- The level and complexity of password setting (on devices, systems, documents).
- Use of USB sticks (e.g. only company owned and encrypted).
- Use of computers, phones and tablets (e.g. company owned versus BYOD, how to react if a device is gone, etc.).
- Use of private cloud/email services/whitelists of private Services and cloud.

To support this setting up a good logical information architecture is necessary. The logical area of the information architecture is where we define 'how' the information concepts are used in practice.

Policies rely on people and behavior and require:
- Clear corporate communication of the defined policies and their purpose throughout the organization.
- Appropriate management conduct.
- Persistent reminder processes surrounding the policies.
- Education of the employees in following the policies.
- Availability and service around devices and functionality.
- Clear definition of roles and responsibilities to ensure that policies are respected and kept up to date.
- Employee contracts reflecting the policies and code of conduct.
- Clearly defined consequences of violating the policies.

5.3.2 Technologies to support PINAM

Identity management system (proactive and preventive)
Ensures that usernames and definitions correlate with actual people.
Ensures that users only have access to the data they need to perform their jobs.
Role based identity management.
Attribute based access control.
Access control systems (proactive and preventive)
Enforces access on operating systems, databases and applications, usually built-in.
Random attacks and viruses will normally not affect as many files if this is in place.
Data tagging system (preventive and reactive)
Meta data assigned to a piece of information.
Categorization and classification of data.
Ensures that you can manage access control, document restrictions, etc.
Enables analysis, e.g. in order to identify if a file contains confidential information.
Firewall discover systems (reactive and preventive)
Data content analysis and discovery.
Event management systems (reactive)
Monitor user activity on critical systems, relate the activity to the person.
Log management.
Behavior analysis. i.e. alert, if someone exports customer details from the CRM.
Mobile Device Management (MDM) (reactive and preventive)
Ensures control of mobile devices, including encryption and locating and/or resetting a device.

5.3.3 How does ISO/IEC 27001 relate to PINAM?
What is ISO/IEC 27001?

"The ISO/IEC 27000 family of standards helps organizations keep information assets secure."

Using this family of standards will help your organization manage the security of assets such as financial information, intellectual property, employee details or information entrusted to you by third parties. ISO/IEC 27001 is the best known standard in the family providing requirements for an information security management system (ISMS).

Source: ISO.org

In other words, it is an information security framework of policies and procedures including all legal, physical and technical controls involved in the organization's information risk management. It includes details for documentation, management responsibility, internal audits, continual improvement, and corrective and preventive action, and enables organizations to manage the security of assets such as financial information, intellectual property, employee details, etc.

Sample planning process for ISO/IEC 27001
- Define a security policy.
- Define the scope of the security management system.
- Conduct a risk assessment.
- Manage identified risks.
- Select control objectives and controls to be implemented.
- Prepare a statement of applicability.
- The standard requires cooperation across all sections of an organization.

■ 5.4 SERVICES AND CLOUD: BYOD (BRING YOUR OWN DEVICE)

> **BYOD** (Bring Your Own Device)
> "BYOD (bring your own device) is the increasing trend toward employee-owned devices within a business. Smartphones are the most common example, but employees also take their own tablets, laptops and USB drives into the workplace."
>
> *Source: whatis.techtarget.com*

Introducing Services and cloud (also known as cloud computing) requires adherence to the PINAM principles. Some best practices:
- Do not deviate from the overall guiding PINAM principles when signing a Services and cloud agreement.
- Also in the cloud, valuable information should be traceable, tagged and monitored.
- Ensure security control and security guarantees.
- Ensure that you have the rights to manage user rights and data restrictions continuously.
- Define ownership of your content, e.g. in case of contract termination: Who owns the data? How and when will it be delivered?

5.4.1 Shadow IT explained

Shadow IT
End-users in the company are using private file sharing solutions such as Dropbox. The solutions are not approved by the IT department, and therefore unmanaged, unmonitored and unsupported.

Shadow IT holds many risks to the organization and needs to be addressed by formulating requirements. An example of a risk is that data stored in these solutions is put at risk of loss and exposure. Addressing the use of shadow IT can be done by formulating consistent policies defining whitelists of solutions and code of conduct around shadow IT. The company must also provide solutions delivering the functionalities that the end users demand, thus avoiding shadow IT.

5.4.2 BYOD considered from the PINAM perspective

In some organizations, BYOD is accepted as 'a fact of modern life'; research has shown that it may increase employee satisfaction and productiveness. But, when adopted, it must be supported!

If BYOD is supported in a company, a PINAM strategy should be implemented setting up policies and regulations such as:
- 'Cleaning' of mobile devices when employees leave the company.
- Mobile security (PIN requirements).
- Responsible conduct.
- Which content can be accessed and shared from the devices?
- How do you track and monitor these devices?
- Security controls.

Risks and requirements
- Many corporate IT users do not know the policies in the company concerning the use of shadow IT and BYOD.
- This indicates that many companies do not have policies or do not communicate or enforce their policies consistently or educate their staff in following PINAM policies correctly.

Exam preparation: Chapter 5

To help prepare for the exam, we have included multiple choice and so-called 'get it' questions (the answer key can be found at the end of this workbook). Additionally, you are provided with an overview of terms you should be familiar with.

Sample exam questions

1. Which are the key benefits of People and Information Asset Management?
   A. Manage and control of end-user license usage.
   B. Managing end-user accounts giving access to business software.
   C. Creating a balance between information agility and information security.
   D. Ensuring that file shares are available and with agreed capacity.

2. What is an important organizational benefit from People and Information Asset management?
   A. Increasing employee satisfaction by ensuring access to right information from any end-user device.
   B. Creating organizational awareness of the value of corporate information and appropriate handling of this.
   C. Ensuring cost control and compliance by tracing software usage.
   D. Initiating internal audit to ensure business processes and procedures are optimized.

3. The PINAM processes and activities can be divided into four main steps. What is not a step in the PINAM processes and activities?
   A. Information categorization versus content restrictions.
   B. Cost control, continuity and compliance.
   C. Policies.
   D. Data tagging and user rights management.

4. Shadow IT may compromise an organization's integrity. In what way?
   A. An end-user is using whitelisted devices to get access to company data and information.
   B. An end-user is using file shares that are unmanaged, unmonitored, and unsupported.
   C. An end-user is using a USB stick that is encrypted, and company owned.
   D. An end-user is using whitelisted software to get access to company data and information.

5. Policies rely on people and their behavior. What is *not* a requirement?
   A. Clear corporate communication of the defined policies and their purpose throughout the organization.
   B. Clear definition of roles and responsibilities to ensure that policies are respected and kept up to date.
   C. Clearly defined processes and procedure to get access to company data and information.
   D. Clearly defined consequences of violating the policies.

'Get it' questions

1. Recall the definition of People and Information Asset Management (PINAM).
Key words: complete lifecycle, policy setting, enforcement, information transparency, people, knowledge, sharing, valuable information, control, data security, user rights, transparency, traceability

2. Name at least four objectives of People and Information Asset Management (PINAM).

3. Name at least four benefits of People and Information Asset Management (PINAM).

4. From a PINAM perspective, what does 'the management of People and Information' refer to?

5. a. What are the four main areas for attention of PINAM?
   b. Name characteristics/principles for each one of these areas.

6. a. Which three additional PINAM principles support productivity?
   b. Explain one of these principles in more detail.
   c. Explain the security restrictions that apply to these principles.

7. Name the four main steps for the implementation of PINAM processes and activities.

8. Explain the two levels at which tagging and management of user rights is addressed.

9. Name at least four technologies that can help support PINAM.

10. Recall the definition of shadow IT and name the risks of and requirements for managing shadow IT.

IT Asset Management Interfaces:
Exam requirements

6. IT Asset Management Interfaces	5 %
6.1 The interfaces of IT Asset Management	
6.2 IT Asset Management roles	

6 IT Asset Management Interfaces

As we stated in Chapter 1, the four key objectives of IT Asset Management are value creation, alignment, leadership and assurance. Alignment is made possible by creating an IT Asset Management ECO system. The best practice process framework that is closest to ITAM and has many overlap areas with ITAM, is IT Service Management (ITSM).

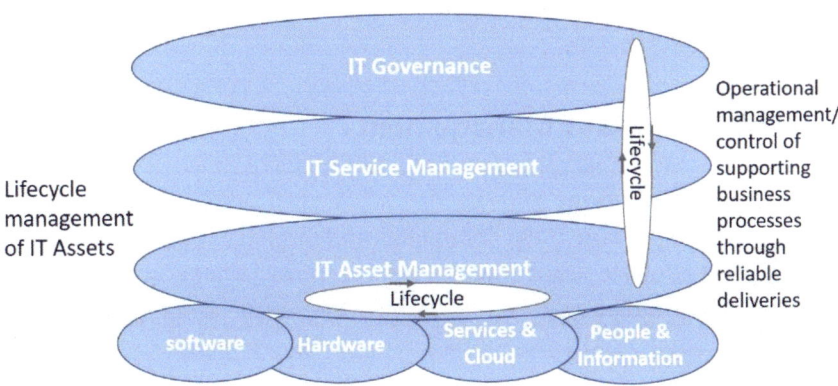

Figure 20. ITAM ECO system and alignment

■ 6.1 THE INTERFACES OF IT ASSET MANAGEMENT

Proper IT Asset Management is made up of a combination of best practice frameworks and standards. ITAM incorporates frameworks and standards for the following four areas:

Asset management:	ISO/IEC 19770 & ISO 55000
IT governance:	ISO/IEC 38500 & COBIT
IT service management:	ISO/IEC 20000 & ITIL
IT information security:	ISO/IEC 27000

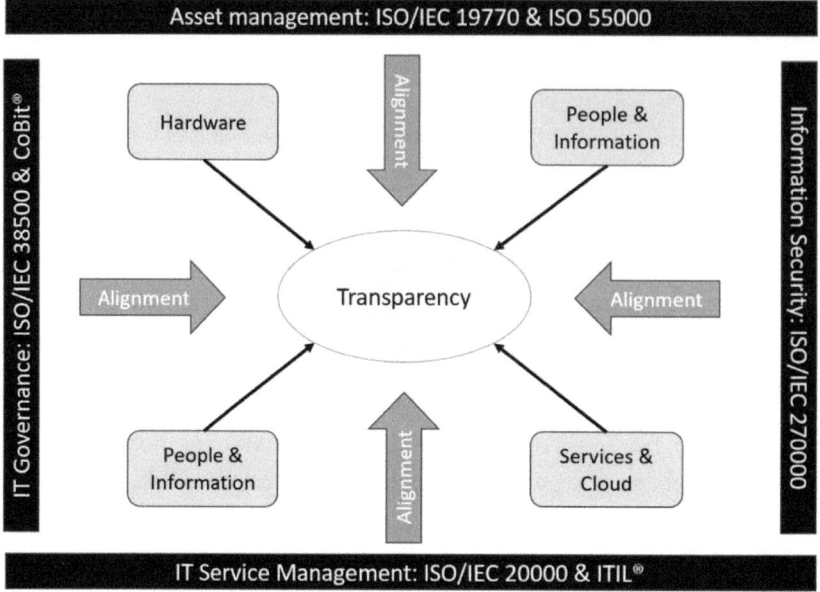

Figure 21. ITAM interface approach

There is a strong alignment between the four areas, and one area cannot be successfully implemented without the others.

6.1.1 Interfaces of IT Asset Management

ISO 55000 - Asset management
The ISO 55000 family of standards help companies and organizations get value from their assets. It sets out the requirements of an asset management system and provides additional useful guidance for applying the standard in practice.

Source: ISO.org

ISO/IEC 19770 - Information technology - Software asset management & IT asset management
The ISO/IEC 19770 family of standards help to establish a baseline for an integrated set of processes for Software Asset Management (SAM), divided into tiers to allow for implementing them and achieving recognition.

Source: ISO.org

ISO/IEC 27000 - Information security management systems

The ISO/IEC 27000 family of standards helps organizations keep information assets secure. Using this family of standards will help your organization manage the security of assets such as financial information, intellectual property, employee details or information entrusted to you by third parties.

Source: ISO.org

ISO/IEC 20000 - Information technology - Service management

ISO/IEC 20000-1:2011 is a service management system (SMS) standard. It specifies requirements for the service provider to plan, establish, implement, operate, monitor, review, maintain and improve an SMS. The requirements include the design, transition, delivery and improvement of services to fulfil agreed service requirements.

Source: ISO.org

ITIL - Best practice framework for IT Service Management

ITIL is the most widely accepted approach to IT service management in the world. ITIL can help individuals and organizations use IT to realize business change, transformation and growth. ITIL is mapped in ISO/IEC 20000. This recognizes the way that ITIL can be used in order to meet the requirements set out for ISO/IEC 20000 certification and the interdependent nature with ITIL.

Source: AXELOS

ISO 38500 - Information technology - Governance of IT for the organization

ISO/IEC 38500:2015 provides guiding principles for members of governing bodies of organizations (which can comprise owners, directors, partners, executive managers, or similar) on the effective, efficient, and acceptable use of information technology (IT) within their organizations.

Source: ISO.org

COBIT - Framework for the governance and management of enterprise IT
The COBIT 5 framework for the governance and management of enterprise IT provides a growth roadmap that leverages proven practices, global thought leadership and tools to inspire IT innovation and help to achieve business success. Topic areas are: audit and assurance, risk management, information security, regulatory & compliance and governance of enterprise IT.

Source: ISACA

6.2 IT ASSET MANAGEMENT ROLES

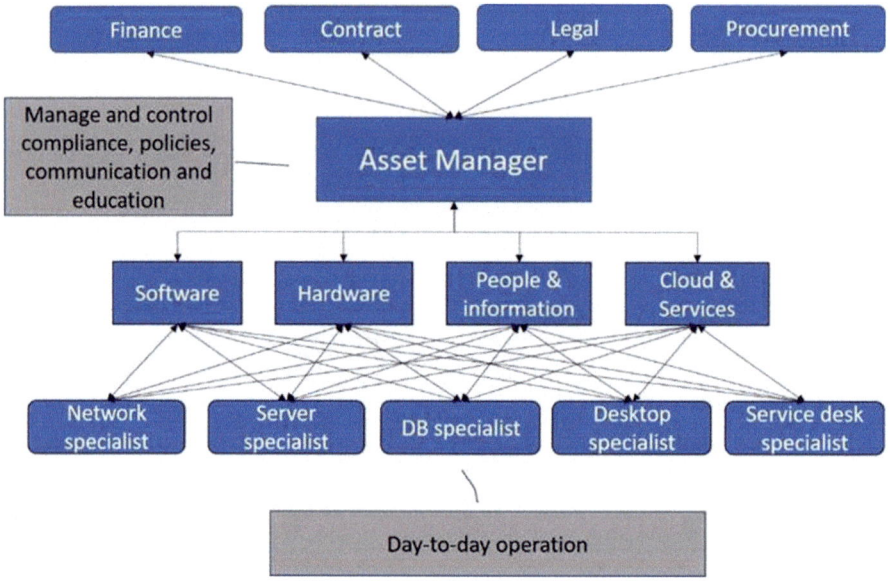

Figure 22. IT Asset Manager's central role

The ITAM ECO system is quite complex and requires support by various roles from within the organization. In this section, we describe the challenges faced by an IT Asset Manager and several prominent roles with which he/she interacts. On the one hand an IT Asset Manager needs to manage and control compliance, policies, communication and education, and on the other hand he/she needs to be involved in and support day-to-day operations.

6 IT Asset Management Interfaces

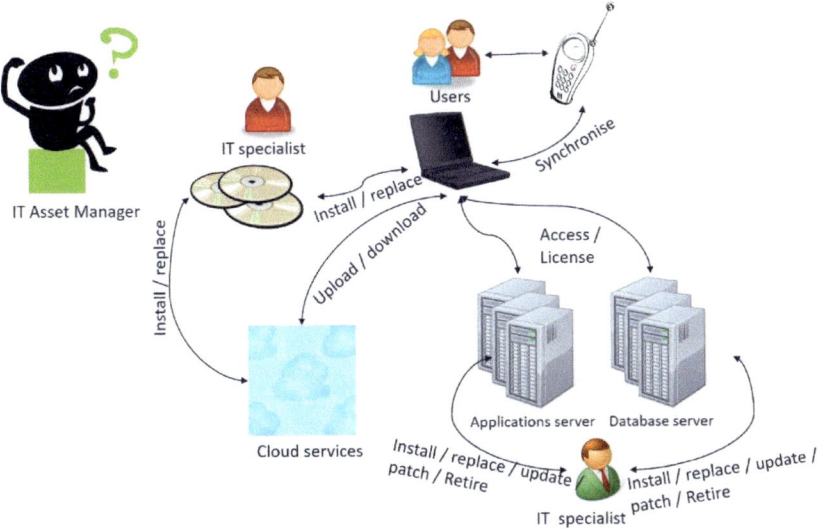

Figure 23. Daily operations involving assets

6.2.1 The challenges facing an IT Asset Manager

An IT Asset Manager has several key tasks in supporting the organization, the ITAM ECO system as a whole, and the different ITAM areas separately. These key tasks are depicted in figure 24.

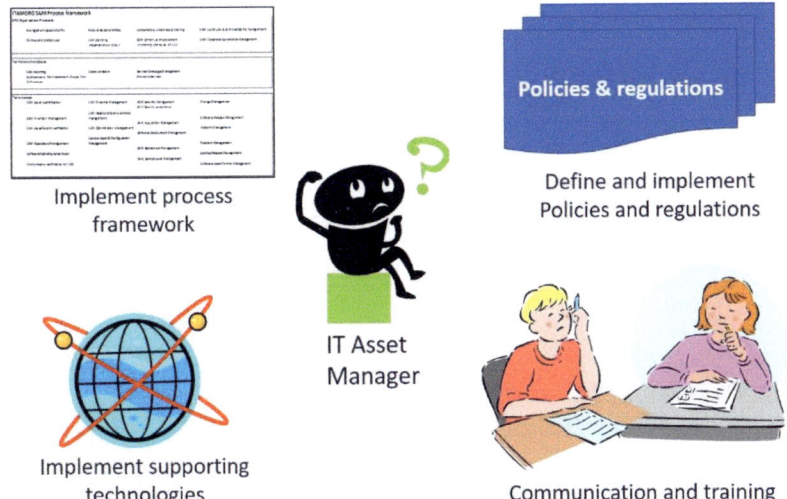

Figure 24. IT Asset Manager challenges

The overlying challenge for an IT Asset Manager is to be in control over all IT assets. However, many other organizational roles are involved with IT assets. See figure 25. Therefore, the IT Asset Manager must involve these roles in the ITAM ECO system. Apart from this involvement, proper processes, procedures and tools need to be implemented. Without these ITAM may prove to be an impossible task.

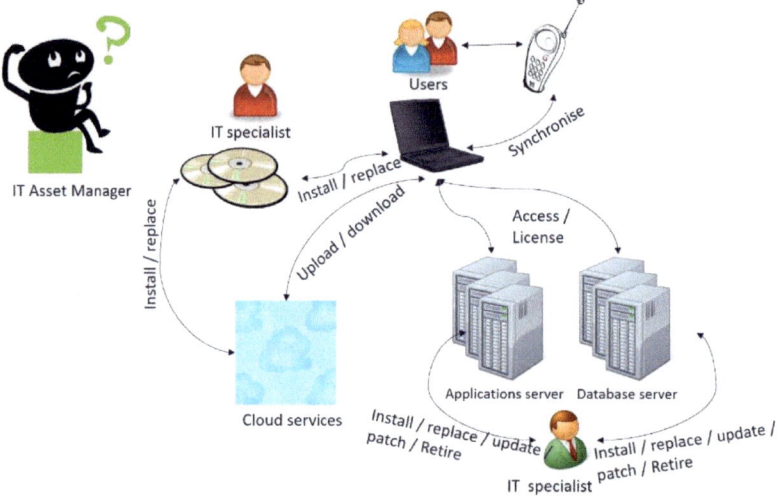

Figure 25. Challenges of related roles

6.2.2 Responsibilities of related roles

Users
Users should be aware of policies (plural) and, confidentiality of information (privacy and data protection). From an IT Asset Manager perspective, there is the responsibility to control and manage people and information, which means:
- Control over user roles and responsibilities.
- Control over granted user rights to applications and Information.
- Management of and control over track and trace of information.
- Being in compliance with Information Security Management.

IT specialists
IT specialists need to be aware of the following issues, when they are carrying out day-to-day operations:
- Terms and conditions.
- Regulation.
- Impact/risk by carrying out day-to-day operations.
- Policies.
- Processes and procedures.
- Harvesting software and licenses when retiring or disposing of hardware.
- Updated and correct inventory and repository.

From an IT Asset Manager perspective, it is important to support the IT specialists. This could be through:
- Education.
- Communication.
- Guidance.

Exam preparation: Chapter 6

To help prepare for the exam, we have included multiple choice and so-called 'get it' questions (the answer key can be found at the end of this workbook). Additionally, you are provided with an overview of terms you should be familiar with.

Sample exam questions
1. IT Asset Management interfaces with parts of the IT ECO system. What framework in the ITAM ECO system should IT Asset Management primarily be aligned with?
   A. To the security management framework because it maximizes the security of using IT assets.
   B. To the application management framework because this framework focuses on the business requirements and needs.
   C. To the project management framework, so it supports the implementation and continual improvement of IT Asset Management.
   D. To the IT service management framework because this plays a major role in managing and controlling the lifecycles of IT assets.

2. It is important that IT specialists are aware of IT Asset Management. How do they best support IT Asset Management?
   A. By ensuring updated and reliable inventory information.
   B. By consulting the IT Asset Manager when deploying new hardware.
   C. By initiating an impact analysis when a change to an IT asset is evaluated.
   D. Making sure that software is licensed correct according to the contractual terms when it is deployed.

3. A new IT Asset Manager has been appointed and must implement proper IT Asset Management in the company. What is the biggest challenge for a new IT Asset Manager?
   A. To produce monthly reporting of software compliance, IT asset usage and IT asset portfolio.
   B. To ensure clear and effective disposal of processes for all IT assets.
   C. To get in control and manage all IT assets in the company in collaboration with all specialists involved across the organization.
   D. To ensure a reliable ITAM tooling system is implemented.

'Get it' questions

1. Name at least one standard or best practice framework for the following four areas of alignment in the ITAM interface approach:

Asset management:	
IT governance:	
IT service management:	
IT information security:	

2. Which best practice framework in the IT Asset Management ECO system has most overlap areas with ITAM?

3. Which international standard helps ITAM to establish a baseline for an integrated set of processes for Software Asset Management (SAM)?

4. Which two of the following four areas of alignment in the ITAM interface approach support alignment with Services and cloud?
Asset management, IT governance, IT service management, IT information security.

5. The ITAM ECO system is quite complex and requires support by various roles from within the organization. Name a few types of daily operations involving assets that have impact on the users (also known as end-users) in the organization.

6. Name the four key tasks of the IT Asset Manager role in supporting the organization.

7. a. Name at least one responsibility for each of the following roles related to the IT Asset Manager:
   - Users.
   - IT specialists.

   b. How can the IT Asset support these roles?
   - Users.
   - IT specialists.

Appendix A List of basic concepts

Terms are listed in alphabetical order.

Basic concepts

Agreement
Assessment
Asset
Asset lifecycle
Asset management
Audit
Baseline
Bermuda Triangle
Best practices
Bring Your Own Device (BYOD)
Change management
Cloud
Compliance
Configuration Management Database (CMDB)
Contract
Contract Manager
Corporate governance
Definitive Software Library (DSL)
Disposal
End User License Agreement (EULA)
Entitlement
Gap Analysis
Governance
Hardware Asset Management (HAM)
Hardware asset management tool
Hardware inventory

Hardware tracking
Hosted applications
Identity management system
Information assets
Information Technology Infrastructure Library (ITIL)
Information security
Infrastructure as a Service (IaaS)
Inventory management
ISO 19770
ISO/IEC 20000
ISO/IEC 27001
ISO 55000
IT asset
IT Asset Management (ITAM)
IT governance
IT infrastructure
Licensing
Lifecycle processes
Lifecycle management
Legalization rules
Managing risk
Mobile devices
Platform as a Service (PaaS)
Policies and procedures
Problem management
Procurement

Procurement manager
Retirement
Risk assessment
Risk reduction
Roles & responsibilities
Security policies
Service desk
Service provider
Services and cloud (outsourcing)
Shadow IT
Software as a Service (SaaS)

Software Asset Management (SAM)
Software asset management tool
Software asset lifecycle
Software audit
Software compliance
Software licenses
Stakeholder
Supplier management
Terms and conditions
UAC (User Account Control) level
Web-based services

Appendix B About ITAMOrg

ITAMOrg is a fast-growing global membership organization of IT Asset Management professionals. With the mission to develop and strengthen the awareness & competencies in IT Asset Management best practices, ITAMOrg offers certified ITAM education. Furthermore, ITAMOrg connects stakeholders in the ITAM ecosystem through knowledge sharing and networking for ITAM professionals from both users and suppliers of IT in order to enable transparency within the industry. For more information, please visit www.itamorg.com

Get more information

ISO19770 (standard for IT Asset Management)
www.iso19770.org

ITIL4 – ITAM practices
https://www.axelos.com/welcome-to-itil-4

ITAM news and feeds
www.itamchannel.com

ITAMOrg memberships and activities
www.itamorg.com

Appendix C Answer Key

Please note that all answer key references are made to the chapters and sections of this workbook.

Chapter 1

Sample exam questions
1. To get success with ITAM, some key components are important. Which key components are important?
   A. Make sure all levels of IT assets are managed and controlled.
   B. Have a good relationship with publishers, vendors, customers, legal and finance.
   C. Have a good knowledge and understanding of goals, the motivation and the key drivers from stakeholders across the organization.
   D. Fulfill stakeholder expectations.

   Feedback:
   A. Incorrect. This is a purpose of the IT Asset Managers purpose, but not a key component.
   B. Incorrect. This is good to have but not a key component for success.
   C. Correct. See Section 1.1.2.
   D. Incorrect. This is only one piece of it, but not all.

2. ISO/IEC 19770 is a standard related to ITAM. What is its purpose?
   A. It is a standard for managing IT assets assisting in managing the risks and minimizing the costs of IT assets.
   B. It is an international standard for People and Information asset management to availability of IT assets.
   C. It is part of best practice guidance within the ITIL framework (Information Technology Infrastructure Library).
   D. It is part of information security management standard (ISO27001) to minimize risks of IT Infrastructure.

Feedback:
- A. Correct. ISO 19770 is the standard for IT Asset Management. See Section 1.2.1
- B. Incorrect. People and Information Asset Management is part of the ISO19770 IT Asset Management standard. There is no specific standard for People and Information Asset Management.
- C. Incorrect. ITIL is a best practice IT Service Management. ISO 19770 is a standard for IT Asset Management.
- D. Incorrect. ISO 27001 is the standard for Information Security and does not include ISO 19770. ISO 27001 and ISO 19770 relate to each other and both Management Systems standards.

3. The CIO/CFO needs to have insight in the IT asset portfolio. Which activities help to get that insight?
   A. The CIO/CFO needs information or needs to be involved about Investment planning and risk & sustainability of IT assets.
   B. Define and continual improvement of the lifecycle and organizational strategic goals.
   C. Insight in the system performance and process control of IT assets.
   D. Utilization of IT assets in the organization.

Feedback:
- A. Correct. Investment planning and risk & sustainability of IT assets are information the CIO/CFO needs to get from the Asset Portfolio level. See Section 1.2.2.
- B. Incorrect. This is what the IT Asset Managers have to define and maintain together with the stakeholders.
- C. Incorrect. This is a part of the responsibility of the IT Asset Manager and is part of the system management of IT assets.
- D. Incorrect. This is important information for the IT Assert Manager to optimize the IT Asset portfolio, and is a requirement to IT operations level.

4. The ITAM process framework is a combination of standards and best practices. Which of the following is most important to enable the ITAM process framework?
   A. Automatic discovery of hardware, database tooling, measure of software utilization.
   B. Risk assessment, business case templates, RACI models.
   C. Request fulfillment of IT asset, automatic deployment of IT assets.
   D. Service management systems, asset discovery, deployment tools.

Feedback:
- A. Incorrect. These are tools within system management which are important for the operational management of IT assets but not part of the enabling of the ITAM framework.

B. Correct. Risk assessment, business case templates, RACI models are important elements to enable the ITAM framework. See Section 1.3.1.
C. Incorrect. IT Service Management and System Management to handle and manage IT Asset but not part of the enabling of the ITAM framework.
D. Incorrect. These are part of the IT Service Management and System Management to handle and manage IT Asset but not part of the enabling of the ITAM framework.

5. To start up an IT asset management program, the IT Asset Manager needs to have insight. What information from a GAP analysis is useful information to the IT Asset Manager to prepare the IT Asset Management program?
   A. A project initiation documentation (PID) plan for the implementation of IT Asset Management.
   B. A list of KPIs to ensure the success of IT Asset Management.
   C. A list of stakeholders and their key roles.
   D. Processes already in place and which can improve the implementation of an IT Asset Management program.

Feedback:
   A. Incorrect. The PID is an outcome of the project planning which the GAP analyses feed information into.
   B. Incorrect. This is part of running an IT Asset Management project which has to define the KPIs.
   C. Incorrect. These are part of the project planning and execution of the IT Asset Management project where the stakeholder's commitment and confirmation are needed.
   D. Correct. Processes already in place are important information to prepare an IT Asset Management program. See Section 1.3.2.

'Get it' questions

1. Recall the definition of IT Asset Management (ITAM).
Key words: strategic, IT assets, lifecycle, practices.
Feedback: See Section 1.1.1.

2. Name at least four objectives of IT Asset Management (ITAM)
Feedback: See Section 1.1.2

3. Name at least four benefits of IT Asset Management (ITAM)
Feedback: See Section 1.1.2.

4. Place the different phases of the ITAM lifecycle in their correct order in the lifecycle model.

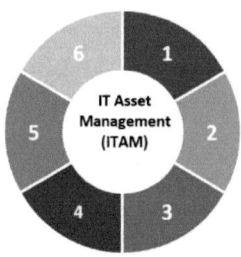

- Receive
- Retire
- Procure
- Request
- Manage
- Strategy/plan

Feedback:

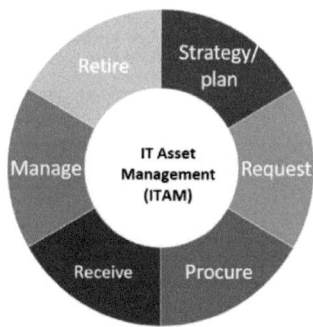

5 a. Explain the so-called 'Bermuda Triangle' of ITAM.
  b. Name some instruments that can help ITAM maintain control over the 'Bermuda Triangle'.

Feedback:
a. "Cooperation between stakeholders is a crucial aspect of ITAM. Another one is maintaining a balance between Requests, Purchasing and Deployment of assets. In ITAM this is called the 'Bermuda Triangle'. The three areas mentioned here are governed by different departments or stakeholders, each with their own objectives and needs."
See Section 1.1.2.

b. "Different instruments can help ITAM to maintain control such as: a predefined software catalogue, service portfolios, a well maintained CMDB to ensure new introductions do not negatively affect the existing infrastructure, purchasing policies and procedures, management of licenses, etc."
See Section 1.1.2.

6. Which best practice models and standards help to create the ITAM best practices?
Feedback:

ITAM Best Practices

Chapter 2

Sample exam questions

1. The software Asset Manager is depending on receiving information/data from the Hardware Asset Manager. What information should the Hardware Asset Manager need to deliver to Software Asset Manager?
   A. A full list of all current processes and procedure used to manage and control IT assets.
   B. A full list of MAC addresses and IP addresses for the related Hardware Assets.
   C. The Hardware Asset Manager need to deliver trustworthy and reliable data of all IT assets in scope.
   D. A list of all valid sources which are used to manage and control IT assets.

   Feedback:
   A. Incorrect. This is not an important information to manage and control software assets.
   B. Incorrect. This is only information relevant for the System Manager in the managing and control of IT Hardware Assets and not relevant data for the Software Asset Manager.
   C. Correct. The Software Asset Manager is depending on trustworthy and reliable data in managing and control Software Assets. See Section 2.2.1.
   D. Incorrect. The list of sources is not needed information for the Software Asset Manager.

2. To prepare a Hardware Asset Management program, what is one of the first decisions you need to take?
   A. How IT Hardware Asset must be managed and controlled.
   B. How to setup the request and procurement process to handle all IT assets.
   C. A definition of the security levels for each Hardware Asset type to be implemented.
   D. A definition and selection of the IT Hardware Asset types included in the scope.

   Feedback:
   A. Incorrect. This is the first decisions but part of the implementation of IT Hardware Asset Management.
   B. Incorrect. The request and procurement processes will be part of the implementation of Hardware Asset Management and are an important part of the managing and control of Hardware Assets.
   C. Incorrect. Security Levels must be defined as part of implementing IT hardware in the infrastructure.
   D. Correct. The Scope of IT hardware to managed is one of the first decisions to take. See Section 2.2.1.

3. What is the correct sequence of the Hardware Asset Management Lifecycle?
   A. Initiation, Design, Build, Migration, Transition, Closing.
   B. Requirements, Design, Implementation, Verification, Maintenance.
   C. Strategy, Design, Transition, Operations, Continual Service Improvement.
   D. Strategy, Request, Procure, Receive, Manage, Retire.

Feedback:
   A. Incorrect. These are steps in the Project Management lifecycle.
   B. Incorrect. These are steps in the Software development lifecycle.
   C. Incorrect. These are steps in the ITIL lifecycle.
   D. Correct. This is the sequence in the Hardware Asset Management lifecycle. See Section 3.2.3.

4. A part of the IT Hardware Asset Managers responsibilities is to manage and control IT hardware assets. Which hardware asset could not be tracked and managed by the Hardware Asset Manager and therefore is potential risk to the organization?
   A. Laptops and printers that are tied to a contract and implemented as part of the operational Infrastructure.
   B. Expensive hardware assets which have been acquired by organization.
   C. Hardware assets support business processes and enable specific value to the business.
   D. Hardware assets that are not owned by the organization.

Feedback:
   A. Incorrect. Hardware assets tied to a contract and implemented should be tracked.
   B. Incorrect. Expensive hardware assets are valuable and acquired by the organization should be tracked.
   C. Incorrect. Hardware assets that support business processes and bring value to the Business, should be tracked.
   D. Correct. Hardware assets that is not owned by to the company, typical Bring Your Own Device (BYOD), cannot be tracked because the company do not have any legal rights to this type of IT hardware and thus not able to fully manage. See Section 3.2.3.

5. IT operation is part of the IT Hardware Asset Management lifecycle and therefore needs to get information and feedback. Which stakeholder is most important for IT operation to receive feedback from?
   A. Contract manager, Software Asset Manager, Financial manager, IT manager, Security manager.
   B. Contract manager, Security manager, Software Asset Manager, Financial manager, Service desk.

C. Financial manager, IT manager, HR manager, Policy manager, Test manager, Service desk.
D. Security manager, Software Asset Manager, Service desk, HR manager, Test manager.

Feedback:
A. Incorrect. Policy manager is not a stakeholder.
B. Correct. These are correct stakeholders. See Section 2.2.4.
C. Incorrect. Policy manager and Test manager are not stakeholders.
D. Incorrect. Test manager is not a stakeholder.

'Get it' questions

1. Recall the definition of Hardware Asset Management (HAM).
Key words: management, portfolio, assets, lifecycle, business decisions, financial objective, value.
Feedback: See Section 2.1.1.

2. Name at least four objectives of Hardware Asset Management (HAM).
Feedback: See Section 2.1.2.

3. Name at least four benefits of Hardware Asset Management (HAM).
Feedback: See Section 2.1.2.

4. Name some benefits of HAM for each of the following stakeholders:
- IT management
- IT operation
- Contract management and Procurement management
- Financial management
- Business.

Feedback:
- IT management
  - Enabling Knowledge based business decisions with respect to procurement, replacement, disposal and re-use of an asset.
- IT operation
  - Agility – short response time; Support the Business
  - Re-use of hardware
  - Use of standard hardware services
- Contract management and Procurement management
  - Request standard services
  - Easier negotiation – standard hardware services

- Financial Management
  - Cost savings – reduction of over-disposal and over-procurement
  - Compliance foundation data
- Business
  - Minimize risk of information

See Section 2.1.2 The purpose and the benefits of HAM.

5. Name some questions that need to be asked for each of the phases of the HAM lifecycle.

Feedback: Typical questions to ask at each stage of the lifecycle are:
1. Strategy/plan: which benefits need to be included (managed) and how are we going to manage them. In which way do we document our assets and how do we support management of assets by tools.
2. Request: who requests the asset and for which purpose? Is the procedure part of an existing service level agreement? Is the asset part of the service catalogue?
3. Procure: what are the costs of buying and maintaining the asset throughout the lifecycle?
4. Receive: when was it received, has it been properly documented? Has it been tested for use?
5. Manage: when and to whom was, the asset deployed? e.g. distribution of 'standard' computer resources, etc. Where is the physical location?
6. Retire: does the asset need to be archived, disposed of or returned to the vendor under the lease contract? Or can it be re-used after refurbishing? What are the regulations for proper disposal?

See Section 2.1.3 Overview of the HAM-lifecycle.

6. By which types of criteria do we determine whether an IT hardware asset should be tracked and managed?

Feedback:
- Financial terms for leasing hardware
- Information about assets needed to manage them
- Information required by stakeholders

See Section 2.2.1 Determining whether an IT hardware asset should be tracked and managed.

7. a. What is the main benefit of using hardware standards?
   b. Name at least five considerations for their use.

Feedback:
a. The main benefit of using these standards is that they enable the management of and control over hardware assets.
b. Considerations for their use:
   - Cost per Asset type – low cost assets will probably not be maintainable.
   - Volume of assets in the organization – One plotter versus 1000 laptops.
   - Asset Lifecycle and depreciation.
   - Security risk.
   - Legal requirements.
   - Asset impact on the productivity.
   - Asset redeployment.
   - Mobility.
   - Business needs per Asset Type.
   - Internal IT Needs per Asset Type.
   - What to put in the Internal and external Service Catalogue.

See Section 2.2.2 Examples of hardware standards and considerations when to use them.

8. What are the main objectives for proper disposal of hardware assets?
Feedback: The main objectives for proper disposal are protection of intellectual property, ensuring software compliance, privacy and data protection, enabling tracking of assets even after disposal, financial (end-of-life status for tax purposes), proper disposal of electronics and hazardous material, minimize risk when IT assets are disposed and it is done cost effectively, and finally support and adapt green strategies. Disposal is part of the 'retirement' stage of the HAM-lifecycle.
See Section 2.2.3 Disposal standards.

9. What are the minimum requirements for a disposal certificate?
Feedback: Needs at least: serial number, data of wiping, Name of the company, LOT number, Sanitation standard used (DoD) – data wiping method, signature.

A lot number is an identification number assigned to a quantity or lot of material from a single manufacturer.
See Section 2.2.3 Disposal standards.

10. a. Name the phases of the hardware lifecycle process.
    b. Name some of the stakeholders that need to provide information to IT operations during this lifecycle.
    c. What information is provided by each of these stakeholders?

Feedback:
a.

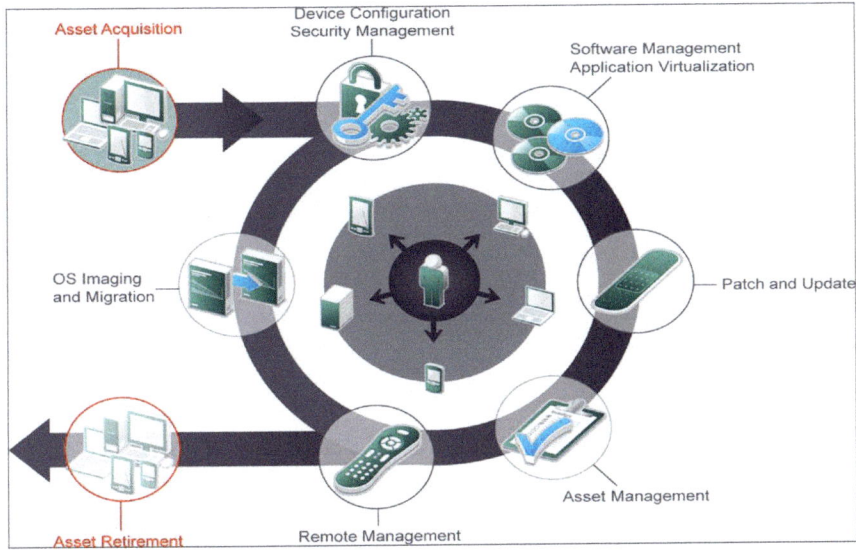

b/c.
- Contract manager: Supplier contracts and terms.
- Security manager: Policies, regulations.
- Software Asset Manager: Software compliance, terms of use.
- Financial manager: Acquisition, disposal, depreciation, hardware forecasts.
- Service desk: Request fulfilment, service offerings.

See Section 2.2.4 The HAM lifecycle in an organization.

11. In what ways can HAM track hardware?
Feedback:
- Network Scanning (IP address, MAC/IMEI)
- RFID scanning
- Tagging Barcode / QR code
- Manual registration.

See Section 2.3.1 Tool considerations for HAM.

12. Explain why Bring Your Own Device (BYOD) is difficult for HAM to manage?
Feedback: Since BYODs are not corporately managed, these devices and their 'control' belongs in the 'People and Information Asset Management' category. BYOD is more and more becoming a grey area because many of these devices are now running corporate apps, and what if a connection is made between a privately owned smart phone and the company's exchange server?
See Section 2.3.2 Mobile device aspects of HAM.

Chapter 3

Sample exam questions

1. Software consists of two essential things, the actual software (functionality) and entitlements. What does an entitlement describe?
   A. How software can be distributed.
   B. The functionality of the software.
   C. How software must be purchased and terms of payment.
   D. The terms and conditions of using the software.

   Feedback:
   A. Incorrect. The distribution of software in an organization is not part of the entitlement.
   B. Incorrect. Software functionality is not part of the entitlement but a separate description of the software.
   C. Incorrect. The purchase of software is not part of the entitlement but is part of the publisher or resellers sales procedure.
   D. Correct. Terms and conditions are used to validate compliance of using the software. See Section 3.1.1.

2. What is the purpose of Software Asset Management?
   A. To prevent personnel to use their own devices to run business software.
   B. To avoid or reduce risk, ensure compliance, and control software costs.
   C. To ensure that software is legally obtained.
   D. To ensure strategic planning and forecasting of software to fulfill the business needs.

   Feedback:
   A. Incorrect. It is not the purpose but is an important thing to include in the software policies.
   B. Correct. The software Asset Manager must control these aspects and that is the purpose of Software Asset Management. See Section 3.1.2.
   C. Incorrect. This is not the purpose, but it is important.
   D. Incorrect. This is not the purpose but part of the operational management of software.

3. When software must be upgraded, this could be a challenge for the IT Software Asset Manager. Which is the most significant challenge?
   A. Specifications and documentation of hardware are not sufficient.
   B. Inflexible and immature installation processes.
   C. Proof of purchase of the software is not documented.
   D. End-users are not educated to use the functionality of the software.

Feedback:
- A. Incorrect. The lack of hardware specification and documentation is a problem the Hardware Asset Manager has to solve, but it will not influence a software upgrade.
- B. Incorrect. This is an operational problem which must be solved either in IT Service Management or system management.
- C. Correct. When software must be upgraded if it is possible to document the proof of purchase of the software. If this is not possible the consequence could be that the organization must re-invest in the new version of the software. See Section 3.2.1.
- D. Incorrect. This is a decision/problem of the business organization and will not influence a software upgrade.

4. A SAM program often fails because of what?
   A. Roles and responsibilities are not clear.
   B. Software cannot be maintained and upgraded.
   C. The software portfolio is outsourced.
   D. Inflexible and immature internal policies.

Feedback:
- A. Correct. No clear Roles and responsibilities for managing and control of Software in place will be a huge problem for the SAM program and often be the reason for a failure. See Section 3.1.2.
- B. Incorrect. This is a huge problem to IT operations with the consequence that they cannot upgrade the hardware infrastructure platform.
- C. Incorrect. Outsourced IT has also to be managed by the Software Asset Manager and it should not influence the Software Asset Management program.
- D. Incorrect. Inflexible and immature internal policies are not a specific problem to SAM.

5. The software publisher (copyright holder) has any right to initiate an audit. What is the purpose of an external software audit?
   A. To verify that the software in use is at the correct version and is aligned with the purpose in the contract.
   B. To verify that the software is used correctly and compliant to the terms and conditions and that licenses have been paid.
   C. To verify that the software being used is in compliance with the general software policies in the organization.
   D. To make sure that software is balanced in relation to the number of licenses purchased.

Feedback:
   A. Incorrect. This is not a reason for the publisher to initiate an external audit but is an issue that should be identified in an internal audit.
   B. Correct. This is the purpose of an external audit. See Section 3.3.1.
   C. Incorrect. This is not a reason for the publisher to initiate an external audit but is an issue that should be identified in an Internal audit.
   D. Incorrect. This is not a reason for the publisher to initiate an external audit but is an issue that should be identified in an Internal audit.

'Get it' questions

1. Recall the definition of Software Asset Management (SAM).
Key words: best practice, software asset, lifecycle, cost control, maintenance, licensing, distribution, documentation.
Feedback: See Section 3.1.1.

2. Name at least four objectives of Software Asset Management (SAM).
Feedback: See Section 3.1.2.

3. Name at least four benefits of Software Asset Management (SAM).
Feedback: See Section 3.1.2.

4. Name at least four attributes that make up a software asset.
Feedback: License information, terms and condition for use, support/service contracts, license keys and authorization codes, release documentation, user manuals, distribution copies (images), master copies and media, number of instances installed (as opposed to the number of licenses, etc.).
See: Section 3.1.1 Defining SAM.

5. Name at least three different stakeholders belonging to the two categories of stakeholders in the SAM stakeholder map.
   1. Internal stakeholders.
   2. External stakeholders.

Feedback:

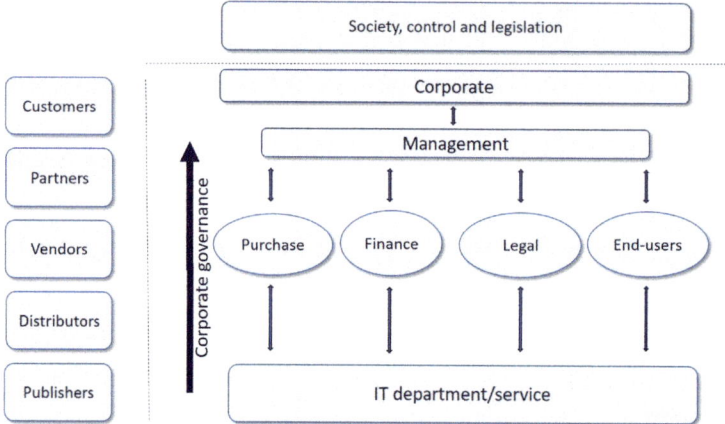

See Section 3.1.4 SAM roles and responsibilities.

6. Name at least five internal SAM roles and their responsibilities.
Feedback:
- Software asset manager: responsible for the management of all software assets during their lifecycle.
- Application manager: responsible for application support and maintenance (including modifications) in cooperation with the vendor. This includes a role in the IT service management processes, especially problem management, change management and release management.
- SAM tool administrator: manages the tools that support the SAM processes and activities.
- Project Manager: manages SAM-related projects.
- Software & license analyst: responsible for tracking and control of licenses.
- Audit manager: quality control and assurance, internal audit, reporting to management and corporate of audit-related information, cooperates with external auditors, creating awareness and ongoing education of staff.
- Software deployment manager: specialist deployment role in large organizations.

See Section 3.1.4 SAM roles and responsibilities.

Appendix C Answer Key

7. What are the stages of the SAM implementation roadmap?
Feedback:

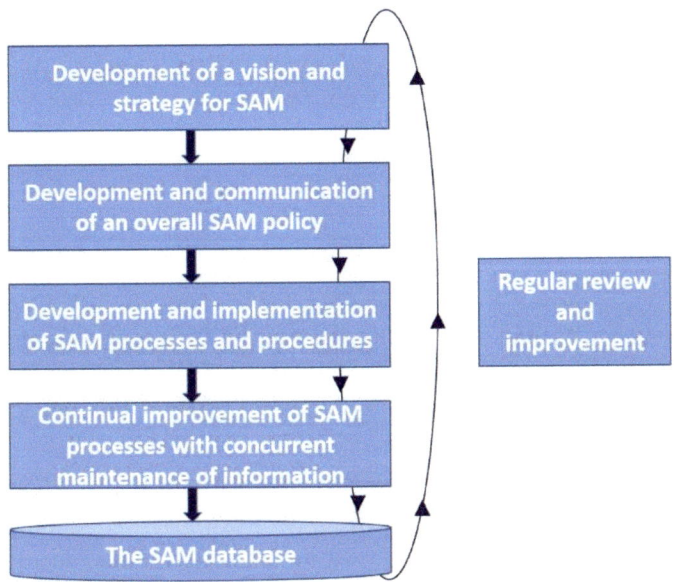

See Section 3.1.5 Introducing SAM best practices.

8. Name the main characteristic of each of the four process tiers in the SAM framework.
Feedback:
The total approach is top-down. Each tier brings specific benefits to the organization, and can be summarized as follows:
- Tier 1: Trustworthy data: Achieving this tier means knowing what you have so that you can manage it.
- Tier 2: Practical Management: Achieving this tier means improving management controls and driving immediate benefits.
- Tier 3: Operational Integration: Achieving this tier means improving efficiency and effectiveness.
- Tier 4: Full ISO/IEC SAM conformance: Achieving this tier means achieving best-in-class strategic SAM.

See Section 3.1.5 Introducing SAM best practices.

9. Name three types of compliance that are specifically important for SAM.
Feedback:
- Licensing compliance: Ensuring that the use of all software within the organization remains within all legal and contractual terms.

- Security compliance: Ensuring that software policies are consistent with security policies and plans.
- Policy and procedure compliance: Ensuring that SAM policies are consistent with corporate policies, strategies and plans.

See Section 3.2 The concept of compliance.

10. Explain how software is sometimes used without licenses being purchased, or proof of license has been lost.

Feedback: Software being used without licenses being purchased or loss of proof of license.

- Software is sometimes installed without going through the complete procurement process or renewal of the authorization (i.e. re-use).
- Proof of purchased licenses may be lost or proof is not official because of purchases from a reseller or after an upgrade of the software
- Lack of understanding of licensing terms and conditions
- Lack of records about software usage and often not even the number of PCs in use

See Section 3.2.1 Violations leading to incompliancy.

11. Give some examples of information that needs to be provided to the auditor(s) of a software audit?

Feedback:
- Hardware and software inventory information.
- Purchasing policies, procedures, records and all related documentation.
- Software usage in relation to licenses and all license information.
- End-user policies.
- Description of asset standards such as software images and their deployment.
- Vendor/reseller documentation such as contracts and invoices.

See Section 3.3.1 Defining audit.

12. Name a few possible consequences that may be brought up by an external audit.

Feedback:
The consequence of a violation or an audit could be:
- Reputational damage: your organization can be 'named and shamed'.
- Security violations: illegal and counterfeit software may cause virus infections, or breaches of personal data may be discovered.
- Down time: a vendor may seize your software assets as part of a court case over a license dispute.
- Delivery up: delivery up is a legal term for "the act of giving something back to someone, especially so that it can be destroyed. Examples include goods produced in breach of intellectual property" (Source: translegal.com).

- Administrative and/or monetary fines: under EU law fines for repetitive damaging breaches of personal data can be punished by monetary fines up to 20,000,000 EUR or up to 4% of the annual worldwide turnover of the preceding financial year in case of an enterprise, whichever is greater (Source: GDPR Article 83, Paragraph 5 & 6).
- Imprisonment: 'worst case scenario'!

See Section 3.3.2 Possible ramifications of an audit.

Chapter 4

Sample exam questions

1. Which one is part of the Agreement terms and conditions?
   A. Clear exit clauses.
   B. User rights and traceability.
   C. Clear SLAs, including data and server delivery terms.
   D. Training and education program.

Feedback:
   A. Correct. Exit clauses is part of Agreement terms and conditions. See Section 4.4.2.
   B. Incorrect. This is a topic for the service agenda.
   C. Incorrect. This is a topic for the service agenda.
   D. Incorrect. This is a topic for the service agenda.

2. Cloud service has a number of benefits. What are the most important benefits from this?
   A. To share servers with other clients is a cheaper solution compared to owning the servers.
   B. Better security and scalability.
   C. Capacity on demand and higher availability of the services.
   D. Agility and scalability of the solution.

Feedback:
   A. Incorrect. Yes, it may be cheaper, but it is not the most important benefit.
   B. Incorrect. Security and scalability are not by definition better.
   C. Incorrect. Capacity on demand and higher availability can be designed as required also for in-house solutions.
   D. Correct. These are the most important benefits. See Section 4.2.2.

3. What is the definition of a Platform as a Service (PaaS) and what does the cloud provider include?
   A. Network, servers, storage & databases.
   B. Computers, virtual machines, databases & firewalls.
   C. Network, servers, storage & tools.
   D. Network, computer, firewalls & virtual machines.

Feedback:
   A. Incorrect. Databases are not part of a PaaS platform but often belong together with business applications. Databases can be operated on that platform but are not a part of what the provider offers.

B. Incorrect. Computers and databases are not part of a PaaS platform.
C. Correct. A PaaS provider offers a platform on which customers can develop, test and run their own business applications. See Section 4.2.1.
D. Incorrect. Computers are not part of a PaaS platform.

4. Before negotiating the contract, which of the following should be included in the pre-analysis ahead of the negotiation?
A. A project plan for the journey/migration into cloud.
B. A plan of practices for maintaining the standards and objectives.
C. Establishing in which areas the business gets added value by moving to cloud services.
D. A plan for how the Business will be impacted by Performance, software, speed time, flexibility, user rights, inventory information, etc, in the future.

Feedback:
A. Incorrect. This is only available after the negotiations.
B. Incorrect. This is only available after the negotiations.
C. Correct. These are the aspects to be included in a pre-analysis. See Section 4.4.1.
D. Incorrect. These are the steps after the negotiations.

5. What is not a possible organizational problem of cloud services?
A. Standard solution did not adjust to the specific needs of the organization.
B. Geographical location of data storage.
C. Enables the organization to focus on the core business.
D. Service provider may change your services beyond your request.

Feedback:
A. Incorrect. This could be an organizational pitfall/problem.
B. Incorrect. This could be an organizational pitfall/problem.
C. Correct. This is an organizational benefit. See Section 4.2.2.
D. Incorrect. This could be an organizational pitfall/problem.

'Get it' questions

1. Recall the definition of Services and Cloud Asset Management (SEAM).
Key words: multiple platforms, environments: cloud, virtual, physical, organizational needs, policies, storage, availability, privacy, data protection.
Feedback: See Section 4.1.1.

2. Name at least four objectives of Services and Cloud Asset Management (SEAM).
Feedback: See Section 4.1.2.

3. Name at least four benefits of Services and Cloud Asset Management (SEAM).
Feedback: See Section 4.1.2.

4. Describe the concept of Services and cloud.
Feedback: Services and cloud (also known as cloud computing) refers to services delivered from a cloud service provider's server, and includes online data storage, backup solutions, web-based services, hosted applications, database processing etc. Cloud computing is a modern form of application hosting 'over the Internet'. Cloud services are generally described as 'anything as a Service or XaaS.
See Section 4.2.1 Services and cloud concept.

5. Name and describe the three main cloud service models.
Feedback:
- **PaaS** – Platform as a service: networks, running servers, storage and tools from the Cloud on which a customer can develop, test and run his own applications.
- **IaaS** – Infrastructure as a service: data center infrastructure on demand. Saves customers capital expenditure because of the pay-per-use model.
- **SaaS** – Software as a service: running software from the cloud including licenses, maintenance (i.e. updates) and support. Potential money saver because of pay-per-use. No unused concurrent licenses are needed.

See Section 4.2.1 Services and cloud concept.

6. What are possible compliance issues for SEAM when using cloud services?
Feedback:
- The cloud provider lets more concurrent users use an application than the actual amount of licenses.
- Unclear license terms and conditions.
- No logging and reporting of software usage.
- Licenses may rely on another layer of resellers.

See Section 4.2.2 The benefits and pitfalls of Services and cloud computing.

7. Describe the 'Triple Play' of SEAM.
Feedback: SEAM is the management of the multiple platforms across physical, virtual and cloud environments with respect to the organizational needs in terms of storage, data protection, policies and availability. This management of multiple platforms across physical, virtual and cloud environments is called the 'Triple Play' of SEAM.
See Section 4.3.1 Defining SEAM.

8. a. What are the two major areas of SEAM processes and activities?
   b. Name at least two tasks for each of these two areas.
Feedback: SEAM processes and activities include two major areas:

- contract negotiations and signing. Tasks:
  - definition of terms and SLAs.
  - Measurements (SLAs) of delivered services.
  - Ensuring that all legal regulations are followed, including license and compliance terms.
  - Alignment of the services and the organization needs in terms of storage, data protection, system capability, policies and availability.
- operational and practical activities after contract signing. Tasks:
  - 'One time' task: Internal workflow - clear definition of roles and responsibilities working within the contract governance.
  - Routine task: Monitoring of SLAs: Service availability, both externally and internally, compliance management and Ensuring data connections and a high-level user interface.
  - Strategic task: Ongoing attention to required adjustments in the service as the organization's needs change.

See Section 4.3.2 The activities of SEAM.

9. Describe some of the questions for the pre-negotiating activity 'pre-analysis'.
Feedback:
- In which areas does our company get added value by this service?
- What are the financial savings and costs in this solution?
- What risks are implied? How can we manage these?
- Any regulations from society that need to be considered?
- Do we have the competencies to negotiate a long-term contract?
- Do we have the resources to manage the contract and to ensure that the contract terms are followed and that the SLAs are met?
- How do we plan the change?

See Section 4.4.1 Pre-negotiation activities.

10. Name some of the possible pitfalls of the contract clause 'Agreement terms and conditions'.
Feedback:
- Clear exit clauses: terms to exit the contract and how to get your data.
- Launch of payments: payment starts upon roll-out and not before!
- Pricing: a fixed price model, including support and access from different regions and platforms and meaningful regulations in e.g. price increases.
- Penalties: services breaches from the provider are tied to financial credits.
- Inventory information: the provider should share all inventory data and have clear agreements.

See Section 4.4.2 Contract clauses and their pitfalls.

Chapter 5

Sample exam questions

1. Which is a key benefit of People and Information Asset Management?
   A. Manage and control of end-user license usage.
   B. Managing end-user accounts giving access to business software.
   C. Creating a balance between information agility and information security.
   D. Ensure that file shares are available and with agreed capacity.

   Feedback:
   A. Incorrect. This is an activity for the Software Asset Manager, not a key point for PINAM.
   B. Incorrect. This is an activity for the IT Access Management team, not a key point for PINAM.
   C. Correct. This is an important key point. See the slide PINAM concept. See Section 5.1.2.
   D. Incorrect. This may be a key point for the IT operation, but not for PINAM.

2. What is an important organizational benefit from People and Information Asset management?
   A. Increase employee satisfaction by ensuring access to right information from any end-user device.
   B. Organizational awareness of the value of corporate information and appropriate handling of this.
   C. Ensure cost control and compliance by tracing software usage.
   D. Initiate internal audit to ensure business processes and procedures are optimized.

   Feedback:
   A. Incorrect. This is not a direct benefit of PINAM it is a benefit of good IT access management.
   B. Correct. This is an important benefit of PINAM. See Section 5.1.2.
   C. Incorrect. This is not a direct benefit of PINAM, but is a benefit for SAM.
   D. Incorrect. This is not a direct benefit of PINAM, but is a benefit for the business.

3. The PINAM processes and activities can be divided into four main steps. What is not a step in the PINAM processes and activities?
   A. Information categorization versus content restrictions.
   B. Cost control, continuity and compliance.
   C. Policies.
   D. Data tagging and user rights management.

Feedback:
   A. Incorrect. This is part of the four steps.
   B. Correct. This is not one of the steps. See Section 5.3.1.
   C. Incorrect. This is part of the four steps.
   D. Incorrect. This is part of the four steps.

4. Shadow IT may compromise an organization integrity. In what way?
   A. An end-user is using whitelisted devices to get access to company data and information.
   B. An end-user is using file shares there are unmanaged, unmonitored, and unsupported.
   C. An end-user is using a USB stick that is encrypted, and company owned.
   D. An end-user is using whitelisted software to get access to company data and information.

Feedback:
   A. Incorrect. Whitelisted devices are company agreed and managed, supported and monitored.
   B. Correct. It has not been selected and tested according to corporate procedures. See Section 5.4.1.
   C. Incorrect. A portable device there is company owned and encrypted will be under control of the IT department.
   D. Incorrect. Approved software is also maintained by the IT department.

5. Policies rely on people and their behavior. What is *not* a requirement?
   A. Clear corporate communication of the defined policies and their purpose throughout the organization.
   B. Clear definition of roles and responsibilities to ensure that policies are respected and kept up to date.
   C. Clearly defined processes and procedure to get access to company data and information.
   D. Clearly defined consequences of violating the policies.

Feedback:
   A. Incorrect. Good communication of policies is a requirement.
   B. Incorrect. Clear definition of roles and responsibilities are important and therefore a requirement.
   C. Correct. Clearly defined processes and procedures are important but not a requirement. See Section 5.3.1
   D. Incorrect. It is important that the consequence of violation the policy is stated and communicated; therefore it is a requirement.

'Get it' questions

1. Recall the definition of People and Information Asset Management (PINAM).
Key words: complete lifecycle, policy setting, enforcement, information transparency, people, knowledge, sharing, valuable information, control, data security, user rights, transparency, traceability
Feedback: See Section 5.1.1.

2. Name at least four objectives of People and Information Asset Management (PINAM).
Feedback: See Section 5.1.2.

3. Name at least four benefits of People and Information Asset Management (PINAM).
Feedback: See Section 5.1.2.

4. From a PINAM perspective, what does 'the management of People and Information' refer to?
Feedback: The management of People and Information refers to data security, access policies and best practices with regard to knowledge and information sharing.
See Section 5.1.1 Defining PINAM.

5. a. What are the four main areas for attention of PINAM?
   b. Name characteristics/principles for each one of these areas.
Feedback:

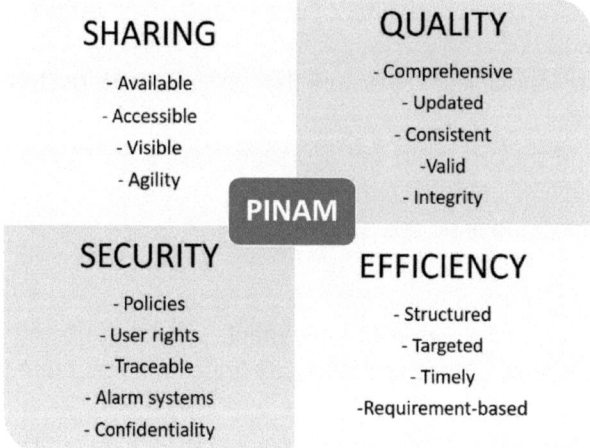

See Section 5.2 / Figure 19: PINAM areas for attention.

6. a. Which three additional PINAM principles support productivity?
   b. Explain one of these principles in more detail.
   c. Explain the security restrictions that apply to these principles.

Feedback:
a. Principles supporting productivity: access anywhere, rich platform for work & cohesive collaboration.
b.
   - Access anywhere: Sharing and managing files from any device.
   - Rich platform for work: Ensuring the ability to interact with any relevant document through tasks, comments, rich preview and clear permissions.
   - Cohesive collaboration: Tightly integrated with everyone's preferred mobile and desktop productivity tools.
c. Restrictions concerning Security: Centralize content into a secure content platform that integrates identity, device and application management toolsets.

See Section 5.2.2 Principles that support productivity.

7. Name the four main steps for the implementation of PINAM processes and activities.

Feedback:
1. Information categorization versus content restrictions.
2. Data tagging and user rights management.
3. Data traceability.
4. Policies.

See Section 5.3.1 PINAM processes and activities

8. Explain the two levels at which tagging and management of user rights is addressed.

Feedback:
Tagging and management of user rights are addressed on two levels:
- Level 1: (manual)
  - Categorization of data; each category gets its own folder
  - Restrict access to specific people/groups
  - … needs policies…
- Level 2: (automatic)
  - Tagging is done by technology.
  - Only when someone tries to access information, user rights are activated.
  - Processes are logged to ensure consistency.

See Section 5.3.1 PINAM processes and activities.

9. Name at least four technologies that can help support PINAM.
Feedback: Identity management system, access control systems (proactive and preventive), data tagging system, firewall discover systems, event management systems, Mobile Device Management (MDM).
See Section 5.3.2 Technologies to support PINAM.

10. Recall the definition of shadow IT and name the risks of and requirements for managing shadow IT.
Feedback: Shadow IT: end-users in the company using private (i.e. unapproved) file sharing solutions such as Dropbox.

Risks and requirements:
- The data stored in these solutions is put at risk of loss and exposure.
- The use of shadow IT must be addressed by consistent policies defining whitelists of solutions and code of conduct around shadow IT.
- The company must provide solutions delivering the functionalities that the end users demand.

See Section.5.4.1 Shadow IT explained.

Chapter 6

Sample exam questions

1. IT Asset Management interfaces with parts of the IT ECO system. What framework in the ITAM ECO system should IT Asset Management primarily be aligned with?
   A. To the security management framework because it maximizes the security of using IT assets.
   B. To the application management framework because this framework focuses on the business requirements and needs.
   C. To the project management framework, so it supports the implementation and continual improvement of IT Asset Management.
   D. To the IT service management framework because this plays a major role in managing and controlling the lifecycles of IT assets.

Feedback:
   A. Incorrect. The security management framework is not the most suitable framework to align with.
   B. Incorrect. The application management framework could be interesting for some aspects but is not the primary framework to align to.
   C. Incorrect. The project management framework is not primarily the framework to align with even it makes good sense to ensure an effective ITAM project.
   D. Correct. The IT service management framework should be closely aligned. See chapter 6: introductory section.

2. It is important that IT specialists are aware of IT Asset Management. How do they best support IT Asset Management?
   A. By ensuring updated and reliable inventory information.
   B. By consulting the IT Asset Manager when deploying new hardware.
   C. By initiating an impact analysis when a change to an IT Asset is evaluated.
   D. Making sure that software is licensed correct according to the contractual terms when it is deployed.

Feedback:
   A. Correct. The IT specialists should ensure this. See Section 6.2.2.
   B. Incorrect. This should be part of the IT change management procedures related to the risk and impact of the IT asset deployment.
   C. Incorrect. This is the job of change management, if required.
   D. Incorrect. This is the job of the IT Asset Manager.

3. A new IT Asset Manager has been appointed and must implement proper IT Asset Management in the company. What is the biggest challenge for a new IT Asset Manager?
   A. To produce monthly reporting of software compliance, IT asset usage and the IT asset portfolio.
   B. To ensure clear and effective disposal processes for all IT assets.
   C. To get in control and manage all IT assets in the company in collaboration with all specialists involved across the organization.
   D. To ensure that a reliable ITAM tooling system is implemented.

Feedback:
   A. Incorrect. To be compliant and to produce a monthly report cannot be done without reliable IT assert data and a good IT governance structure.
   B. Incorrect. These are activities that are part of the job, but not the biggest challenges.
   C. Correct. To get in control and to level with his peers is the biggest challenge. See Section 6.2.1.
   D. Incorrect. The IT Asset Manager will not be in control simply with a tool. A tool in itself does not solve the issues.

'Get it' questions

1. Name at least one standard or best practice framework for the following four areas of alignment in the ITAM interface approach:

Asset management:	
IT governance:	
IT service management:	
IT information security:	

Feedback:

Asset management:	ISO/IEC 19770 & ISO 55000
IT governance:	ISO/IEC 38500 & COBIT
IT service management:	ISO/IEC 20000 & ITIL
IT information security:	ISO/IEC 27000

See: Section 6.1 The interfaces of IT Asset Management.

2. Which best practice framework in the IT Asset Management ECO system has most overlap areas with ITAM?

Feedback: Alignment is made possible by creating an IT Asset Management ECO system. The best practice process framework that is closest to ITAM, and has many overlap areas with ITAM is IT Service Management (ITSM).
See: Chapter 6 (introductory section).

3. Which international standard helps ITAM to establish a baseline for an integrated set of processes for Software Asset Management (SAM)?
Feedback: ISO/IEC 19770.
See Section 6.1.1.

4. Which two of the following four areas of alignment in the ITAM interface approach support alignment with Services & Cloud?
Asset management, IT governance, IT service management, IT information security.
Feedback: IT service management, IT information security.

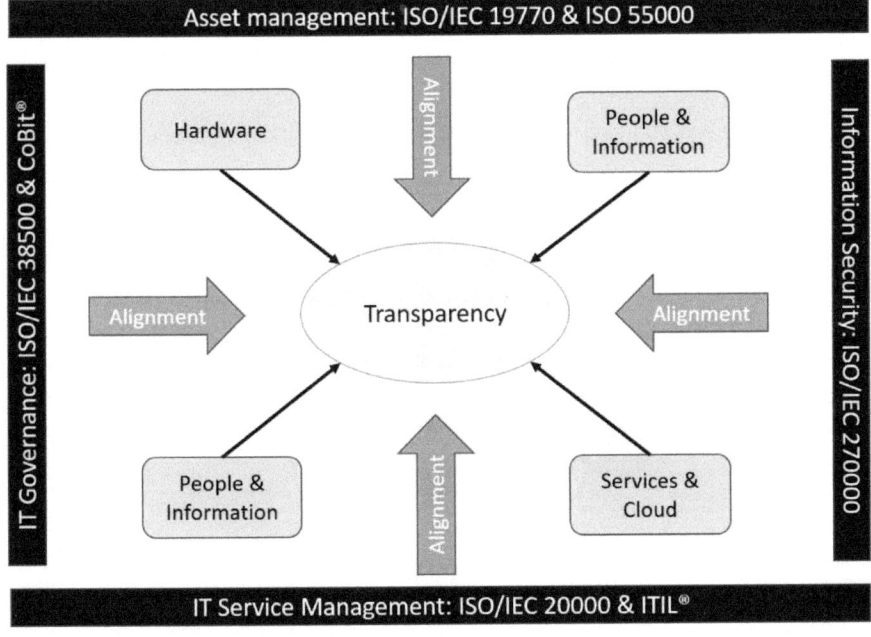

See Section 6.1 The interfaces of IT Asset Management.

5. The ITAM ECO system is quite complex and requires support by various roles from within the organization. Name a few types of daily operations involving assets that have impact on the Users (also known as end-users) in the organization.
Feedback:

See Section 6.2 IT Asset Management roles.

6. Name the four key tasks of the IT Asset Manager role in supporting the organization.
Feedback:

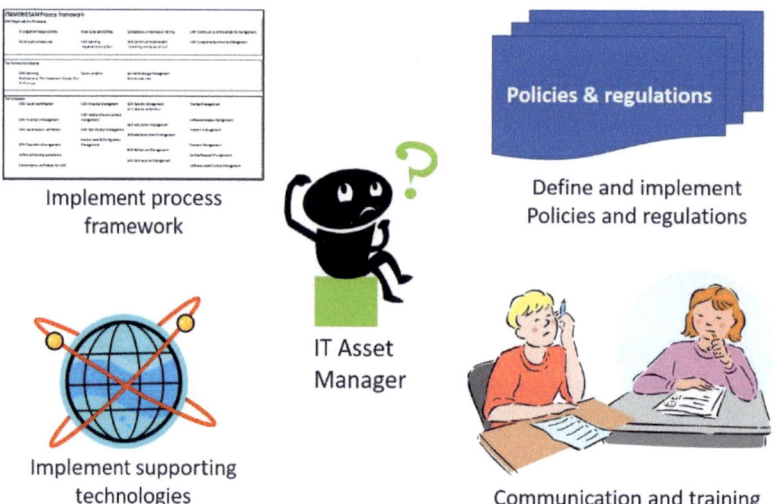

See Section 6.2.1 The challenges facing an IT Asset Manager.

7. a. Name at least one responsibility for each of the following roles related to the IT Asset Manager:
   - Users.
   - IT specialists.

b. How can the IT asset support these roles?
- Users.
- IT specialists.

Feedback:
a/b. Users
Users should be aware of:
- Policies, policies, policies.
- Confidentiality of Information.

From an IT Asset Manager perspective, there is the responsibility to control and manage people and information, which means:
- Control over user roles and responsibilities.
- Control over granted user rights to applications and Information.
- Management of and control over track and trace of information.
- Being in compliance with information security management.

a/b: IT specialists
IT specialists need to be aware of the following, when they are carrying out day-to-day operations:
- Terms and conditions.
- Regulation.
- Impact/Risk by carrying out day-to-day operations.
- Policies.
- Processes and procedures.
- Harvesting software and licenses when retiring or disposing of hardware.
- Updated and correct inventory and repository.

From an IT Asset Manager perspective, it is important to support the IT specialists, this could be through:
- Education.
- Communication.
- Guidance.

See Section 6.2.2 Responsibilities of related roles.